PRAISE FOR 15-MINUTE STEM BOOK

In a world in which our children will increasingly be expected to possess skills [...]
thrive and flourish as adults, this inspirational book is a must-have for any pri[...]
for parents with young children. Emily Hunt has collected 40 imaginative, eng[...]
activities that will open up the minds of our young people.

> Bobby Seagull, school maths teacher, author of *The Life-Changing Magic of Numbers*
> and co-presenter of the BBC's *Monkman & Seagull's Genius Guide to Britain*

Emily Hunt does it again! *15-Minute STEM Book 2* is a must-have resource for busy teachers wanting to implement meaningful hands-on STEM learning. It offers highly engaging activities that walk you through the challenge, beginning with the set-up and materials and ending with connections to STEM careers as well as the concepts behind each activity. Your students will beg for more!

> Carly and Adam Speicher, STEM Curriculum Developers at Carly and Adam LLC

15-Minute STEM Book 2 offers a wide range of inexpensive, hands-on activities to stoke young children's engagement and develop their transferable soft skills as they explore new ways of thinking and doing.

The book features an amalgamation of well-known and loved activities as well as new ones (e.g. the Ocean Plastic Problem) that let the children lead their learning, while the hook questions will also be very effective in generating excitement and sparking debate. Furthermore, the 'What are we learning?' explanations will allay some adults' potential concerns about not knowing the answer, offering them a valuable scaffold with which to answer the children's questions on the subject.

> Dr Lyn Haynes, Senior Lecturer in Education and Science Tutor (Teach First Programme),
> Canterbury Christ Church University

Emily has compiled a perfect book for teachers and families looking for simple STEM activities to do with young children. There are 40 ideas that can be done in any home or classroom using everyday resources. Plus, each challenge has career connections and ideas for further exploration. Get this book for every parent and teacher you know!

> Chris Woods, teacher, speaker, STEM nerd and author of *Daily STEM*

This book is crammed with loads of exciting and challenging learning opportunities to really get children hooked into STEM subjects. It offers engaging activities with clear instructions, and the beautiful illustrative photography makes it clear that we can all get stuck in, get mucky and develop our creative and logical thinking.

15-Minute STEM Book 2 is just the resource to get kids excited for learning, and it will prove to be a treasure trove of ideas for the busy teacher.

> Martin Illingworth, Senior Lecturer in Education,
> Sheffield Hallam University and author of *Forget School*

Emily Hunt

15 MINUTE BOOK 2 STEM

More quick, creative Science,
Technology, Engineering and Mathematics
activities for 5–11-year-olds

Crown House Publishing Limited
www.crownhouse.co.uk

First published by
Crown House Publishing
Crown Buildings, Bancyfelin, Carmarthen, Wales, SA33 5ND, UK
www.crownhouse.co.uk

and

Crown House Publishing Company LLC
PO Box 2223, Williston, VT 05495, USA
www.crownhousepublishing.com

British Library of Cataloguing-in-Publication Data

A catalogue entry for this book is
available from the British Library.

Print ISBN 978-178583507-0
Mobi ISBN 978-178583524-7
ePub ISBN 978-178583525-4
ePDF ISBN 978-178583526-1

LCCN 2020948423

Printed and bound in the UK by
Charlesworth Press, Wakefield, West Yorkshire

CONTENTS

ACKNOWLEDGEMENTS

It has been incredibly heart-warming to see the activities in *15-Minute STEM* come to life in the homes and schools of readers across the country. The opportunity to continue the series with a second book was too good to miss!

To the team at Crown House Publishing, thank you again for sharing my enthusiasm for STEM education and for your guidance throughout the process. It has been a pleasure to work with you once more.

To Jane Hewitt, whose wonderful photography brings each activity to life, thank you for all your hard work. Thanks also to Leonie, Tommy, LJ and Alex for their involvement in testing and modelling many of the activities.

This book was written in a time of unique global and personal challenges: in the midst of the COVID-19 pandemic and while on maternity leave with my newborn son, George. In a year marked by school closures and social distancing, parents and educators have been thrown in at the deep end with home learning. Suddenly, everyday items have been seen in a new light, as meaningful resources to bring learning to life. Learning about big ideas from ordinary objects is the very essence of the 15-minute STEM approach and I hope this book serves as a useful and inspiring resource for many.

INTRODUCTION: MAKING REAL-WORLD STEM CONNECTIONS IN JUST 15 MINUTES

STEM (science, technology, engineering and mathematics) will play a crucial role in shaping our futures. From the digital revolution to the construction industry, from caring for our environment to space exploration, STEM industries continue to grow at a rapid rate and many young people will go into STEM-related jobs. STEM skills will be instrumental to meeting some of the biggest global challenges, as set out in the UN's sustainable development goals.[1]

STEM education is a captivating, inspiring way of connecting educational experiences to real-life opportunities. It's a cross-disciplinary approach with problem solving at its heart. In starting with a real-world problem or question we make the activity relevant to children's lives, helping them to make connections between what they are learning, *why* they are learning it and how they could use it in the future.

But then again, if you've picked up this book, the chances are you already know all of that. Perhaps you've already enjoyed *15-Minute STEM*[2] and are back for more quick, easy-to-resource STEM activities. If you haven't, then you may well be looking for answers to one or all of the following questions:

How do I get children excited about STEM education?

What equipment do I need?

How do I introduce the 15-minute STEM activities?

How can children learn STEM skills in just 15 minutes?

Is 15-minute STEM purely about science, technology, engineering and maths?

15-Minute STEM Book 2 is compiled of 40 quick, easy-to-resource activities for primary school teachers and is also ideal for parents to use at home with their children. Each activity can be made suitable for ages 5–11 with a little bit of adaptation. The activities have been tested to ensure that they take just 15 minutes, although some require a little advanced preparation or need to be returned to later in the day – these are clearly indicated. This means that with minimal preparation you can slot them into those spare moments in an otherwise busy day.

The photographs in this book were taken during the COVID-19 pandemic. Due to school closures and social distancing restrictions only a small number of children could be used to illustrate the activities. We look forward to featuring more children in the images for subsequent reprints when restrictions allow.

---

1   https://sdgs.un.org/goals.

2   Emily Hunt, *15-Minute STEM: Quick, Creative Science, Technology, Engineering and Mathematics Activities for 5–11-Year-Olds* (Carmarthen: Crown House Publishing, 2018).

How do I get children excited about STEM education?

Hook children in with a real-world problem or question

Each activity begins with a hook question, designed to generate excitement and spark debate. These hooks can be found below the title of each activity. They are worded as a question that a child might ask themselves and make real-world links to a diverse range of areas, from natural disasters to robotics. Wording the hook questions in this way helps to contextualise the learning, giving the activity a real-world purpose and helping children to see the practical application of the skills and learning involved. The diversity of the hook questions also gives you the flexibility to select an activity based on – for example – a particular area of interest, a topical issue or a current area of learning.

What equipment do I need?

Keep your resources simple

When we think of STEM education, we often think of expensive equipment such as 3D printers, computers and robotics kits. In reality there are lots of fantastic STEM activities that can be resourced using everyday materials found at home or in the classroom, allowing you to deliver them at short notice. By keeping the resources simple and familiar, we encourage children to think more creatively about how to use them. The 'You will need' boxes outline the resources you will need to complete each activity once. You will need a set of resources for each child or group undertaking the activity.

How do I introduce the 15-minute STEM activities?

Let the children lead the learning

Pose your hook question, expose the children to the resources and then step back and let them lead the learning. So often we 'teach' children how to do activities, guiding them through each step to help them avoid mistakes. Instead, the 15-minute STEM instructions are written as a script that can be delivered directly to the children, and you'll notice that these instructions are on the lighter side. I'd encourage you to be hands-off with the children, supporting where needed with guidance and encouragement.

How can children learn STEM skills in just 15 minutes?

Know your key takeaway points

While we want to encourage children to lead the learning, it's also important to end each activity with a shared understanding of what we have learnt. Therefore each activity is accompanied by a 'What are we learning?' box which provides a simple, child-friendly explanation of the activity, reassuring you that you don't need to be an expert to deliver high-quality STEM education. You may find that an activity introduces a new concept, or it may help to consolidate an area of prior learning by encouraging your child or class to put their knowledge into practice within a real-world context. Stick to the basic structure of the activity with younger children and use the 'Investigate' cues to extend the task with older children.

Is 15-Minute STEM purely about science, technology, engineering and maths?

Each activity develops soft skills

When we step back and let children solve problems themselves, we provide a fantastic opportunity for them to develop soft skills. Critical thinking, problem solving, confidence, creativity, the list goes on ... These soft skills are crucial to success in STEM, as well as in other careers. You will see from the icons at the top of each page that many of the activities have the option to be completed in teams. This provides children with an excellent opportunity to develop the skills of teamwork and communication, for example. The activities also give children opportunities to make mistakes in a safe, supportive environment, enabling them to develop the important skill of resilience. Remind them that mistakes are an important part of the learning process, they're inevitable and, often, they're an important milestone on the way to something greater.

Oh, and another thing ...

15-minute STEM activities link to future careers

Each activity is linked to two STEM careers that engage with conceptually similar tasks, a glossary of which is included at the back of the book. Research shows that the perceptions children have about certain jobs and careers are formed at a young age and that gender stereotyping exists from the age of 7.[3] By introducing children to relevant STEM careers we can challenge these early perceptions and stereotypes and widen their career aspirations. Giving children activities that expose them to the world of work from an early age isn't daft; it's helping to give them the best start in preparing for their futures. When children are learning something, they should be thinking about *why* they're learning it.

Now, let's get started!

3 Nick Chambers, Elnaz T. Kashefpakdel, Jordan Rehill and Christian Percy, *Drawing the Future: Exploring the Career Aspirations of Primary School Children from Around the World* (London: Education and Employers, 2018). Available at: https://www.educationandemployers.org/wp-content/uploads/2018/01/Drawing-the-Future-FINAL-REPORT.pdf.

HEALTH, SAFETY AND A FEW OTHER BITS

- Some activities come with templates or resources for you to copy (e.g. activity 13, Hot Air Balloon Flight), but you might want to have a go at making your own instead.

- Some of the activities are seasonal. For example, activity 28, Rainbow Leaf Walk, works best in the autumn when there are lots of fallen leaves. Save these activities for the right time of year.

- Some of the activities are messy! It's a good idea to try them outside and to make sure that you are wearing suitable clothing. This is indicated at the start of these activities – see the key below.

- Some of the activities need to be returned to throughout the day (e.g. activity 33, Shadows and Sundials). Again, this is noted at the start of these activities.

- Some of the activities require a small amount of advanced preparation (e.g. for activity 40, Winter Coats, you will need to have a tray of ice cubes frozen ready).

- Some of the activities involve the use of single-use plastics. Where possible, reuse these plastics for other activities.

Some important guidelines to share with the children:

- When working with warm water, take it from the hot tap rather than a boiling kettle.

- When doing outdoor activities, remember to stay within sight of an adult.

- Take care with sharp objects, such as scissors.

- Never taste any of the products of the experiments.

- Wash your hands after completing each experiment and be careful not to touch your eyes.

- Be respectful of the natural environment, being careful not to disturb it.

- When working with living creatures such as minibeasts, make sure they are returned to where they are found.

Throughout the book you'll find different icons next to the activities. Here's what they mean:

 You will need to return to these activities later in the day to make observations or collect more results.

 These activities can be done individually.

 These activities can be done inside.

 These activities are also suitable for teams.

 These activities are best done outside.

 Be extra safety-conscious with these activities; adult help or accompaniment may be necessary.

Best done outside

Can be done individually

Suitable for teams

1. ANIMAL CAMOUFLAGE WALK

How do animals protect themselves from predators?

You will need

- A camera, or phone/tablet with a camera
- A magnifying glass
- A timer

How to do it

1. Decide on an outdoor setting for your walk (e.g. a woodland, a field, a playground).

2. You have just 15 minutes to find and photograph as many examples of animal camouflage as you can find. See if you can find examples from across different animal groups (e.g. birds, mammals and arthropods, which includes insects).

3. Use a magnifying glass to investigate each animal further. Try looking closely at tree trunks, leaves and flowers, and within leaf litter.

4. When the time is up, review the findings and count how many examples you photographed.

Optional: Now select a different outdoor setting and see if you can find different examples of animal camouflage.

Investigate

The military often uses camouflage to protect its people and equipment from observation by enemy forces. See if you can find three examples.

What are we learning?

Some animals protect themselves from predators by blending into their surroundings using camouflage. Examples of this might be a grey squirrel against tree bark, a moth on a wall or a green shield bug on a leaf. Other animals use colour to make them stand out as a defence against predators. Examples of this are the red of a ladybird or the black and yellow stripes of a bee. This is called 'warning colouration' and signals to any potential predators that the animal is too costly to attack and eat, because it may be poisonous or aggressive.

Biologist

Naturalist

Can be done inside

Can be done individually

2. BALLOON HOVERCRAFTS

How can we reduce friction using air?

You will need

- A balloon
- A CD
- A push-up sports bottle cap
- Sticky tack

Investigate

Now vary the amount of air in the balloon to see how this affects its speed of travel.

How to do it

1. Push the bottle cap down into the closed position and place it in the middle of the CD, over the hole, securing using sticky tack.

2. Inflate the balloon and stretch the opening to place it over the bottle cap.

3. Position your hovercraft on a flat surface, lift the bottle cap (inside the balloon) up into the open position and watch your hovercraft move. You may need to give it a gentle nudge to get it started!

4. Now test your hovercraft on a range of different surfaces (e.g. table, carpet, concrete playground). On which surface does your balloon hovercraft move fastest? On which is it slowest?

What are we learning?

Friction is a force that is created when surfaces rub against each other. The balloon releases air, creating an air cushion beneath the CD. Without this air cushion the CD would have experienced far more friction if you had given it a gentle push to help it move across a surface and this would have slowed it down. Smoother surfaces (e.g. a polished floor) create a better air cushion than rougher surfaces (e.g. a carpet), allowing the balloon hovercraft to travel faster. Real hovercrafts create a cushion of air beneath them, drastically reducing frictional forces, and have propellers to drive them forwards across surfaces such as water or ice.

Mechanical engineer

Physicist

Can be
done inside

Best done
outside

Can be done
individually

Suitable for
teams

3. BEAVER DAMS

Why do beavers build dams?

You will need

- A tray
- Water
- Natural materials (e.g. sticks, stones and sand)
- A jug

Investigate

Research one of the world's most famous dams (e.g. the Hoover Dam in the USA or the Three Gorges Dam in China).

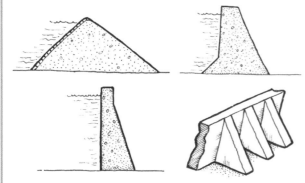

How to do it

1. Begin with a tray, half-filled with water. This represents a river. For this activity you will need to imagine that you are a beaver, living on the river. Your challenge is to build a dam on the river to create a still area of water for you and your family to live in.

2. Collect natural materials (e.g. sticks and stones) that you could use to construct a dam.

3. Use these materials to build a dam wall across the middle of the river that will store the water, creating a still pool for your beaver family.

4. Slowly pour water from a jug into one end of the tray to represent the river flowing down from upstream. Does the dam work in stemming the flow of water? If not, how could you improve your design?

What are we learning?

A dam is a barrier that restricts the flow of water in a river. Beavers are accomplished engineers who build dams on rivers using natural materials, creating a still pond to call their home. They are far more comfortable on water than they are on land, so a dam provides protection against predators and easy access to food. They use their strong teeth to gnaw through tree branches to add to the walls of their dam. There are four main types of man-made dam: embankment, gravity, arch and buttress. They are built from concrete or natural materials, such as rocks and earth, and are created to suppress floods or to store water for uses such as irrigation or drinking. We can also obtain electricity from the water through hydroelectric power, as water flows with the force of gravity to turn water turbines.

Water engineer

Environmental engineer

Best done outside

Can be done individually

Suitable for teams

Be extra safety-conscious

4. BOTTLE ROCKETS

How do rockets propel themselves into space?

You will need

- Bicarbonate of soda
- Vinegar
- A dessertspoon
- A plastic bottle (or reusable plastic water bottle)
- A cork or rubber bottle stopper
- Decorative materials (e.g. cardboard, tinfoil, sticky tape)
- A cardboard cereal box
- Scissors
- A paper towel
- Protective goggles (optional)

How to do it

Note: This activity should take place outside and requires adult supervision. You should stand well back for the rocket launch and may want to wear protective goggles.

1. Begin by decorating your rocket (plastic bottle), ready for launch. For example, you could add cardboard wings. The opening of the bottle will need to be at the bottom (i.e. the bottom of your bottle is the top of your rocket).

2. Take a cardboard cereal box and position it horizontally on the ground to create your launch pad. You will need to cut out a hole in the middle of the box for the rocket to sit in. The hole should be slightly wider than the diameter of your bottle stopper.

3. Insert the bottle stopper into the rocket and place it on the launch pad. Ensure that the bottle stopper is elevated slightly off the floor.

4. Remove the bottle stopper and half-fill your rocket with vinegar.

5. Place two dessertspoonfuls of bicarbonate of soda onto your paper towel and fold the towel around it as though you are wrapping up a present. This helps to delay the reaction so you have time to get out of the way.

6. Place your paper towel inside the bottle, insert the bottle stopper and then place it on the launch pad, standing well back, ready for launch!

Investigate

Experiment with different quantities of bicarbonate of soda and vinegar to see which propels the rocket furthest into the air (you will need to estimate this by sight). Find out how much fuel was needed to get to the moon.

What are we learning?

When we add bicarbonate of soda and vinegar together a chemical reaction takes place. The acid in the vinegar reacts with the bicarbonate of soda, creating bubbles of carbon dioxide. Adding the bottle stopper creates pressure inside the bottle until it is so great that the stopper pops out, the gas escapes, and the rocket launches into the air. In a real rocket the engines create huge amounts of thrust from burning rocket fuel, ejecting gases to propel the rocket into space. This is an example of Newton's third law in action: for every action (gas escaping downwards) there is an equal and opposite reaction (rocket being pushed upwards). This upward force (thrust) is greater than the gravitational force on the rocket (weight), so there is lift-off. Full-scale rockets require enormous amounts of fuel.

Aerospace engineer

Astronaut

13

Best done outside

Can be done individually

5. BUG COUNT

What bugs live in different habitats?

You will need

- A hula hoop
- A magnifying glass
- A clipboard
- Paper and a pencil
- Insect identification book or app
- A timer

Investigate

Now conduct the same activity in a different local habitat. What is similar about your results? What is different?

How to do it

1. You are going to conduct a survey to find out what minibeasts are living in the outdoor space around you. However, the space is too big to survey it all so you will need to use a hula hoop to help you.

2. Place your hula hoop down onto a patch of open ground (e.g. an area of field, garden or woodland floor). Begin the 15-minute timer and then kneel down and see what minibeasts are inside the hoop. Use your magnifying glass to take a closer look and an identification book or app to look up the insects you find.

3. Each time you discover a minibeast, record it on a piece of paper. A tally chart is a useful way of doing this.

4. When you have recorded all the minibeasts in your hoop, use any remaining time to pick it up and place it onto a new patch of ground within the same outdoor area. Then carry out a new survey and compare your findings. Are your results similar? If not, can you explain why they might be different?

What are we learning?

A habitat is an area that provides an animal or plant with food, water, shelter and space to live in. It is likely that you discovered that there are lots of minibeasts living within the patch of habitat that you surveyed. Imagine how many there must be in the entire area – too many to look at them all individually. Scientists often carry out biodiversity studies to discover the number of different species of plants and animals in a particular habitat. Surveying helps them to identify important information, such as threatened or endangered species. To do this they break the area down into smaller plots, like we did with our hula hoop. You may have noticed that the minibeasts you found varied depending on where you placed your hula hoop down. There are lots of reasons for this, including the availability of food, shelter and water nearby.

Entomologist

Statistician

Can be
done inside

Suitable for
teams

6. CODED MESSAGES

How can we share messages over long distances?

You will need

- Paper and a pencil
- Morse code resource (see page 16)
- A medium to communicate your message, such as:
  - Light (e.g. torches)
  - Sound (e.g. a musical instrument such as a xylophone)
  - Electricity (e.g. a battery, two crocodile clip leads and a light bulb)

Investigate

Research the famous Enigma encryption machine, which was used by the Germans to send secret messages during the Second World War. Find out about the role that mathematician Alan Turing played in cracking the code.

How to do it

Note: It would be helpful to take a quick look at the activity resource to help you learn the basics of Morse code before beginning this activity.

1. We need to pass on a very important message, but the other person is too far way for us to shout it!

2. Look at the Morse code resource: each letter of the alphabet is translated into a series of dots and dashes.

3. Decide on your message and select the items that you will use to communicate it. Your partner may wish to use paper and a pencil to record the message.

4. Share your message with your partner, using your chosen method of communication to convey each letter as a series of dots and dashes. Remember to leave a gap equivalent to three dots between letters and a gap equivalent to seven dots between words. Was your partner able to successfully decode it? If so, swap over and pass on a new message to each other.

Optional: Younger children could be given a word to communicate; older children could be given a short sentence. Alternatively, they could choose their own message.

What are we learning?

Morse code encodes the letters of the alphabet into a series of dots, dashes and spaces. Developed in the 1830s, it was named after Samuel Morse, the inventor of the telegraph, and was usually transmitted using the on-off of an electrical current. Morse code messages are not secret, because the coding system is publicly known. However, they can be made secret using encryption, as they were during the Second World War. Nowadays, much of our digital communication is encrypted: converted from plain text into an unreadable 'ciphertext' using a known encoding system and a 'key' known only to the sending and receiving devices. This makes it difficult or impossible for people without the key to read or listen to our communications, even if they intercept them.

Cryptographer

Electrician

Morse Code Resource

- One dash is equivalent to three dots.
- The gap between letters is equivalent to three dots.
- The gap between words is equivalent to seven dots.

A •–	J •–––	S •••
B –•••	K –•–	T –
C –•–•	L •–••	U ••–
D –••	M ––	V •••–
E •	N –•	W •––
F ••–•	O –––	X –••–
G ––•	P •––•	Y –•––
H ••••	Q ––•–	Z ––••
I ••	R •–•	

Can be done inside

Can be done individually

7. COLOURFUL CHROMATOGRAPHY

How can we separate the colours in ink?

How to do it

1. Half-fill a selection of cups with water.

2. Take a coffee filter or piece of kitchen roll and draw a ring in the middle of it using a coloured felt-tip pen. Then place it into one of the cups so that the middle is slightly submerged in the water.

3. Repeat this process using a different coloured pen on each coffee filter or piece of kitchen roll. Place each one into a different cup of water.

4. Stand back and watch the water travel up the material, causing the colours to run and separate.

5. Which colours gave the most impressive results? Why do you think this is? Did any of the results surprise you?

Investigate

Find four different makes of black pen and repeat the experiment. Is each black pen made of the same coloured dyes?

What are we learning?

The water travels up the coffee filter or kitchen roll by a process called capillary action. This is the ability of water to flow through narrow spaces, even upwards against gravity, thanks to the forces of cohesion (water molecules are attracted together) and adhesion (water molecules are attracted to and stick to other substances). We see this same process take place in plants when they draw water up through their roots and stem.

The technique of separating chemical mixtures in a laboratory is called chromatography. The ink in each felt-tip pen is created from a mix of different dyes. The different parts of the ink mixture (dye chemicals) travel at different speeds through the coffee filter, causing them to separate. Chromatography can be used for a range of different purposes, from identifying biological materials to finding clues at crime scenes.

Biologist

Forensic scientist

Can be done inside

Can be done individually

8. COOKIE EXCAVATION

How do archaeologists discover and retrieve artefacts without damaging them?

You will need

- A raisin or chocolate chip cookie
- A paper towel
- Small 'excavation tools' (e.g. toothpicks and tweezers)
- Recording grid resource (see page 19) and a pencil

Investigate

Research the difference between an archaeologist and a palaeontologist. Find out about the famous archaeological site Sutton Hoo and its artefacts in the British Museum.

How to do it

1. Begin by placing your cookie onto the recording grid resource and drawing around the outside. This shape represents your excavation area.

2. Place the cookie onto a paper towel, ready to begin the excavation. You will be working as archaeologists to uncover the artefacts (chocolate chips or raisins) hidden within the excavation area (cookie). Just like archaeologists, you must work slowly and carefully to ensure that each artefact remains in one piece.

3. Use the toothpicks or tweezers to carefully remove each chocolate chip or raisin, one at a time. As you do so, record the location by placing a small dot or cross in the corresponding area of the coordinates grid.

4. When your excavation is complete, take a look at the recording grid resource. Are the artefacts clustered together or spread out?

Optional: Older children may be able to read the coordinates of each artefact. These are written along the X and Y axes of the recording grid. They could also add further detail to the coordinates grid, such the size and depth of each artefact.

What are we learning?

Archaeologists work on excavation sites to remove earth in order to find buried artefacts. An artefact is something made by humans in the past, such as tools or works of art. Archaeologists work slowly and carefully, using tools such as small trowels and brushes for delicate items, as large spades might cause damage. Each time they encounter an artefact they stop and map it on a grid system so that they have an accurate record of where it was found on the site. This is known as the archaeological context and shows what other artefacts were found nearby. The grid system divides the ground into small squares, usually marked with rope or string. Archaeologists also record the depth of each artefact. Geology is applied to understand the natural and human influences on the land, such as how the soil has been used for agriculture.

Archaeologist

Geologist

Cookie Excavation Resource

	A	B	C	D	E	F	G	H	I	J
10										
9										
8										
7										
6										
5										
4										
3										
2										
1										

Return to
activity later

Can be
done inside

Can be done
individually

Suitable for
teams

9. EARTHQUAKE-PROOF STRUCTURES

How can we design a building to survive an earthquake?

You will need

- A tray
- Jelly
- Spaghetti
- Marshmallows

Investigate

Find out more about the design and materials used to build some of the world's most iconic earthquake-proof structures (e.g. the Burj Khalifa, Taipei 101 or the Petronas Towers). Find a map showing the famous San Andreas Fault.

How to do it

Note: You will need an adult to prepare a tray of jelly (with a depth of approximately 3 centimetres) in advance to make sure that it is set for the activity.

1. You are going to create a building, but you need to think carefully about its design because the area is prone to earthquakes!

2. Build your structure on a flat surface (e.g. a table) using marshmallows and spaghetti. Use the marshmallows as joins by digging the spaghetti into them. Remember to make sure that the base is small enough to fit on the tray of jelly.

3. Once complete, place your building in the centre of the tray of jelly. You may wish to build a foundation by inserting spaghetti into the jelly base.

4. Wobble the tray to create an earthquake! Did your structure survive? If not, how could you improve it to make it more earthquake-proof?

Optional: What is the tallest structure you can create that is still earthquake-proof?

What are we learning?

Earthquakes are mostly caused by the sudden movement of the earth's tectonic plates (these are large pieces of the earth's outer shell). As one plate tries to move past the other, pressure gradually builds up until they suddenly slip. This releases large amounts of pent-up energy as seismic waves, which spread out from the plates' boundaries (the 'fault line') as an earthquake. Seismologists are scientists who study earthquakes, recording their strength and size using the Richter magnitude scale. Some parts of the world are particularly prone to earthquakes, and architects and engineers have to take this into consideration when designing buildings. They design buildings to be flexible enough to withstand some limited side-to-side movement. Methods include reinforcing the structure with cross braces and horizontal frames, placing the building on flexible foundations, or adding shock-absorbing cylinders or counter-swinging pendulums in skyscrapers.

Civil
engineer

Seismologist

Best done
outside

Suitable for
teams

10. EMERGENCY SHELTERS

How can we provide shelter for people after a natural disaster?

You will need

- Paper
- Scissors
- Thin cardboard (e.g. cereal boxes)
- Sticky tape
- Plastic carrier bags/bin bags/plastic sheeting (or biodegradable bin bags)
- Watering can
- Water

How to do it

1. There has been a natural disaster and many people have been left homeless. They need shelter from the rain, quickly! However, there are limited resources available so you must use cheap, lightweight, easy-to-resource materials.

2. Roll the paper and cardboard into tubes, secure with tape, and use these tubes to construct the frame for the shelter. It needs to be big enough for one person to sit inside.

3. Once the frame is complete, cover it with plastic sheeting such as carrier bags to help to weather-proof it.

4. Now it's time to test it! Pour water across the top using a watering can. Did your shelter withstand the force of the rain? Did the person inside get wet? How could you improve your shelter to make it more effective?

Investigate

Japanese architect Shigeru Ban created emergency shelters using recycled cardboard tubes to house disaster victims. Find out more about him and his architecture.

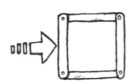  

What are we learning?

Natural disasters such as floods or earthquakes can create urgent housing shortages if they damage or destroy buildings. In this situation, aid organisations and governments help to provide quick-response emergency shelters such as tents. Tents are not especially durable, so architects and environmental engineers have been experimenting with more dependable, low-cost designs. These include bamboo-framed huts, paper-framed shelters (much like ours), shipping containers, and prefabricated, flat-pack houses with solar panels for electricity. You may well have found that the most successful paper shelter designs will probably include triangles. Triangles are inherently rigid. This means that when we apply a force to them, they don't change their shape (unlike, say, a square, the corners of which may shift).

Architect

Environmental engineer

Can be done inside

Can be done individually

11. FIZZING COLOURS

What happens when we mix oil and water?

You will need

- A small plastic bottle (or reusable plastic bottle)
- Food colouring
- Cooking oil
- Water
- Effervescent (fizzing) tablets (e.g. effervescent vitamin C)
- A torch (optional)

How to do it

1. Take your plastic bottle and half-fill it with cooking oil.

2. Then fill the rest of the bottle with water. Add in a couple of drops of food colouring.

3. Screw the lid onto the bottle and give it a shake. What do you notice happens when the oil and water mix?

4. Now remove the lid and add a fizzing tablet. Watch the colourful bubbles rise!

Optional: Shine a torch upwards from the bottom of the bottle for a lava lamp effect.

Investigate

Try screwing the lid back on the bottle after adding the fizzing tablet. What happens to the size of the bubbles? Experiment with the temperature of the water to see how it affects the reaction (but remember, don't use boiling water).

What are we learning?

Oil has a lower density than water, so it floats to the top of the bottle. Density is the mass of an object divided by its volume. To put it another way, it measures the amount of matter contained a given space.

The fizzing tablet contains citric acid and sodium bicarbonate (bicarbonate of soda). When you drop the tablet in water, the acid and the bicarbonate of soda react. This creates bubbles of carbon dioxide that disrupt the liquids in the bottle, pushing some of the oil temporarily lower down and creating a lava lamp effect as it floats back up again.

Chemist

Product designer

Can be done inside

Can be done individually

12. GEODESIC DOMES

What is a geodesic dome?

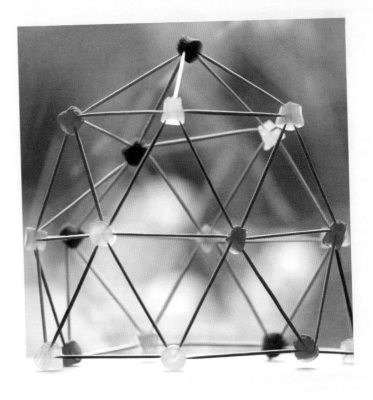

You will need

- Cocktail sticks
- Gummy sweets or plasticine

Investigate

Research some famous examples of geodesic domes, such as the Eden Project in Cornwall or the Spaceship Earth structure at Walt Disney World Resort in Florida.

How to do it

Note: It may be helpful to look at a few images of geodesic domes before you begin to construct your own.

1. Begin by creating a triangle with three equal length sides (an equilateral triangle) out of cocktail sticks, using the gummy sweets or plasticine to join them together at the corners.

2. Continue to create equilateral triangles, joining them together to create the base of your geodesic dome.

3. Once you have created your base, build the triangles upwards, tessellating them together to form a dome shape.

Optional: Once you have made a dome, see if you can turn it into a geodesic sphere.

What are we learning?

Geodesic domes are three-dimensional, sphere-like structures with flat polygon faces, straight edges and sharp vertices (corners). The polygon faces (outer surfaces) of a geodesic dome are equilateral triangles. The triangles are structurally rigid and distribute stress throughout the dome. Geodesic domes tend to be lightweight and easy to assemble. Another benefit of using them is that they can cover large areas without needing internal columns to help support the weight of the structure. The American architect R. Buckminster Fuller was a famous advocate of geodesic domes, building his own 'Dome Home'. They have been less popular for ordinary housing because it is harder to add features like windows and internal partitions for rooms. They have been used in the design of planetariums, stadiums, theatres and churches.

Architect

Civil engineer

Can be
done inside

Can be done
individually

Be extra safety-
conscious

13. HOT AIR BALLOON FLIGHT

How do hot air balloons fly?

You will need

- Balloon panel template (see page 25)
- Tissue paper
- A pencil
- Scissors
- Glue or sticky tape
- A hairdryer
- A timer

Investigate

Experiment with changing the shape of the balloon by adjusting the panels. Can you create a more efficient design?

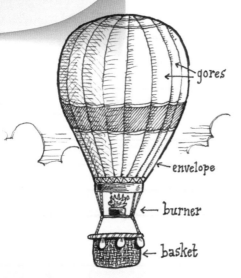

gores

envelope

burner

basket

How to do it

Note: You may need adult supervision when using the hair dryer.

1. Use a pencil to trace the hot air balloon panel template onto tissue paper. Then carefully cut it out.

2. Repeat this process until you have five tissue paper panels.

3. Stick the second tissue paper panel to the tabs of the first one. Continue to add each of the panels. Finally stick panel five to panel one to create your completed balloon envelope.

4. Hold the balloon envelope above a hair dryer (this is acting as the burner). Turn the hairdryer on and watch your balloon fly! How long can you keep your balloon in the air for?

What are we learning?

In a real hot air balloon flight, the envelope of the balloon is filled with hot air from the burner above the basket. The burner uses propane, which is a gas under normal pressure but can be compressed into a liquid and stored in cylinders in the basket. After the burner flame is ignited by a pilot light (a small flame), the burner coils heat up – which preheats the propane before it leaves the cylinders. This ensures that it vaporises fully into a gas and burns powerfully, warming the air inside the balloon. Hot air is less dense than the cool air surrounding it, causing the balloon to rise. The pilot can control the height of the hot air balloon by igniting the burner to make it rise higher or by releasing hot air from a vent at the top of the balloon to make it descend. The ideal weather conditions for a hot air balloon flight are good visibility, no rain, and winds of less than 10 miles per hour.

Aerospace
engineer

Pilot

Balloon Panel Template

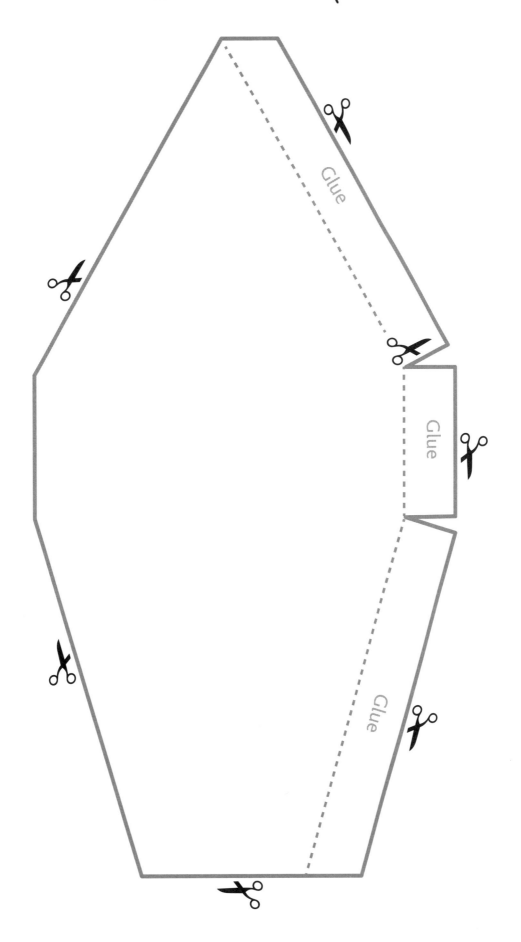

Return to activity later

Best done outside

Can be done individually

14. HOT COLOURS

How does colour affect heat absorption?

You will need

- Clear glasses or jars (which are all the same size) x5 (minimum)
- Paper in a selection of different colours (including black and white)
- Water
- Rubber bands
- A measuring jug
- A thermometer
- Paper and a pencil (optional)

Investigate

Use the internet to look for images of buildings that have used colour to either reflect or absorb light. See if you can find an example from a hot climate and one from a cold climate.

How to do it

Note: This activity is best done on a sunny day. You will need to keep returning to it to see the results.

1. Wrap a layer of coloured paper around the sides of the first glass or jar, securing it in place with a rubber band. Leave the top of the jar uncovered.

2. Repeat until each glass or jar is wrapped in a different coloured piece of paper.

3. Fill each glass or jar with the same amount of water, at the same temperature, and position them outside in direct sunlight.

4. Return at regular intervals to measure the temperature of the water in each container using a thermometer. Which container has the coolest water? What colour paper is wrapped around it? And the hottest?

Optional: Use paper and a pencil to record your results as you go.

What are we learning?

Different colours reflect energy from sunlight to a greater or lesser extent. At the boundary of the paper and the glass surface, some of the light waves are absorbed – this transfers the energy into the glass, which warms the water. Some of the light wave will also transmit (pass) through the paper and glass into the water, which also contributes to warming. Dark colours – such as black – reflect little light and absorb more, so this makes the water in the glass heat up quicker. Lighter colours – especially white – reflect more light, keeping the water in the glass cooler for longer. Buildings in hot climates are often designed in light colours. Light coloured roofs in particular help reflect the sun's warmth and keep the building cooler. Likewise, buildings in colder climates are often constructed from darker materials, or painted in darker colours, to help absorb heat and to passively warm the inside of the building.

Physicist

Product designer

Can be done inside

Suitable for teams

Be extra safety-conscious

15. HURRICANE HOUSES

How can we design a house to survive a hurricane?

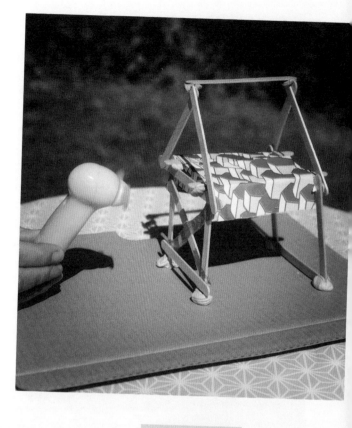

You will need

- Paper
- Lolly sticks
- Plasticine and sticky tape
- Scissors
- A tray
- A fan
- A timer
- A tape measure

Investigate

A typhoon is a type of tropical cyclone. Find a globe or a world map and identify the intertropical zone, between the Tropic of Cancer and the Tropic of Capricorn: this is where tropical cyclones originate.

How to do it

1. You are going to be creating a house with one key design requirement: to be hurricane-proof! Before you begin, quickly decide on a building strategy. You will need to give particular thought to the height and the shape of the house.

2. Start the 15-minute timer and set to work building your house. Use lolly sticks to create the frame and plasticine or sticky tape to join it together.

3. Check that your house is secure in preparation for high winds. This includes checking that your structure has firm foundations by using plasticine or sticky tape to secure it to the ground (tray). Use paper to cover the walls and roof, sticking it in place.

4. Time is up! Place your house in front of the fan – 1 metre away – and turn it on. If it withstands the winds for 30 seconds without blowing away or getting damaged, start moving it forward in 10-centimetre increments (steps). You could refer to these as hurricane categories, with the closest increment to the fan representing a 'Category 5' storm with the highest wind speeds.

Optional: Experiment by building houses of different shapes and sizes and reflect on why some are more successful than others.

What are we learning?

Tropical cyclones are rapidly rotating storms. 'Cyclone' refers to the circular motion, and 'tropical' to their usual origin over tropical seas. Such storms are called different things depending on their strength and on where in the world they occur. In the Atlantic Ocean and north-eastern Pacific Ocean, cyclones are called hurricanes. Hurricane have wind speeds of at least 74 miles per hour and are most common between June and November. At the centre of the hurricane is the eye, an area of very low pressure where the wind is calm. The most dangerous part of the hurricane is the wall around the eye. The strength of the storm is categorised from 1 to 5, with 5 being the strongest (defined as wind speeds of over 157 miles per hour). Circular building designs help to reduce wind pressure. If high winds are blowing onto a rectangular building, there would be the risk of the pressure being too great on one side. Hurricane-resistant building designs often include concrete walls and a sloped roof to deflect the wind.

Civil engineer

Meteorologist

Best done
outside

Suitable for
teams

Be extra safety-
conscious

16. KNOTTED PROBLEM

What is the strongest type of knot?

You will need

- String
- Scissors
- A bucket with a handle
- A measuring tape
- Weight to add to the bucket (e.g. water, rice, sand, books)
- Knot resource (see page 30)
- Gloves (optional)

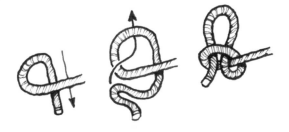

Investigate

Knots are used in lots of areas of life, including camping, sailing, mountaineering and fishing. Pick one of these areas and find out more detail about the types of knots that are used.

How to do it

Note: You will need adult supervision when working with string to make sure that it is used safely. You could wear gloves as an extra safety precaution when holding the string to lift the bucket.

1. The challenge is to create the strongest knot you can. You will test this by seeing how much weight the knot can hold when you use it to suspend a bucket.

2. Cut a piece of string to a length of 30 centimetres. Look at the knot resource and choose a knot to recreate. The overhand knot is a simple one to start with.

3. Tie one end of the string to the handle of the empty bucket using your chosen knot. Make sure that you follow the diagram on the knot resource carefully.

4. When the knot is secure, place the empty bucket on the ground and add your chosen weight until it's a quarter full. For example, pour in some of the water. Carefully lift the bucket off the ground for a few seconds using the unknotted end of the string. Does the knot hold?

5. Continue to fill the bucket with your chosen weight in quarterly increments (steps). Remember to put the bucket down between each test of strength. Be careful in case the knot fails and the contents of the bucket escape!

6. When you have tested the first knot, repeat the activity with another one. Can it hold more or less weight?

What are we learning?

There are a large variety of knots and each has properties that make it suitable for different tasks. Knowing the purpose of each type of knot and when to use it is a useful skill. There are situations when using the wrong knot can be very dangerous. We often use a common overhand knot to tie our shoelaces. Other common knots include the clove hitch, which is used to secure rope to a tree or post: useful for campers to secure tent pegs. The bowline knot is popular among mountaineers, climbers and sailors. This is because the knot doesn't slip, regardless of the load applied. The strongest knot is thought to be the constrictor knot because it is so difficult to untie once tightened. It is often used by surgeons to stitch up wounds: it is important for healing that the stitches are very secure.

Doctor

Sailor

Knot Resource

Overhand knot

Slip knot

Clove hitch

Half hitch

Bowline

Reef knot

Resource from *15-Minute STEM Book 2* © Emily Hunt, 2020

Available to download from www.crownhouse.co.uk/featured/15-minute-stem-2

Can be
done inside

Can be done
individually

17. MARSHMALLOW CONSTELLATIONS

How do astronomers use stars to divide up the night sky?

You will need
- Marshmallows
- Cocktail sticks or spaghetti
- Black paper or fabric
- Constellations resource (see page 32)

How to do it

1. Take a few minutes to look at some of the different constellations found in the night sky using the constellations resource.

2. Choose a constellation that you would like to recreate using marshmallows and cocktail sticks.

3. Put your constellation together, pushing the cocktail sticks or spaghetti firmly into the marshmallows to secure them.

4. Display your constellation against a black background.

Optional: If you are working with others who have also completed this activity, can you identify each other's constellations? What shapes can you see within the constellations?

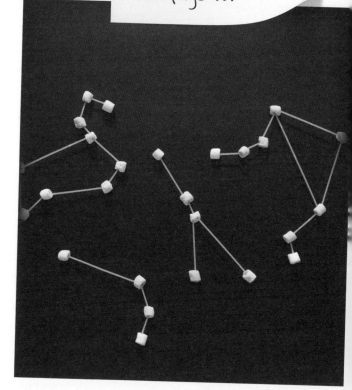

Investigate

Find out what constellations are currently visible in the night sky, then have a go at recreating them with marshmallows and cocktail sticks or spaghetti. If you are in the northern hemisphere, look at the night sky for the Plough (also called the Big Dipper). This is part of the Ursa Major constellation. If you are in the southern hemisphere, try to find the Southern Cross (Crux).

What are we learning?

A constellation is a group of stars in a recognisable (but imaginary) pattern. Modern astronomers divide the sky into regions of stars using 88 constellations. Many of the constellations were named by Greek astronomers after mythological people, creatures or inanimate objects. From our point of view, the sun, moon and planets in our solar system appear to travel around a narrow path in the sky called the ecliptic path. This runs directly through the 12 famous constellations that we call the zodiac. Some constellations shift with the seasons, while others can only be seen depending on where you are on earth: in the northern or southern hemisphere. (We sometimes see the signs of the zodiac referred to as 'star signs'. This is called astrology and is the idea that stars can have an influence over our lives. Unlike astronomy, astrology has no scientific validity.)

Astronomer

Astronaut

Constellations Resource

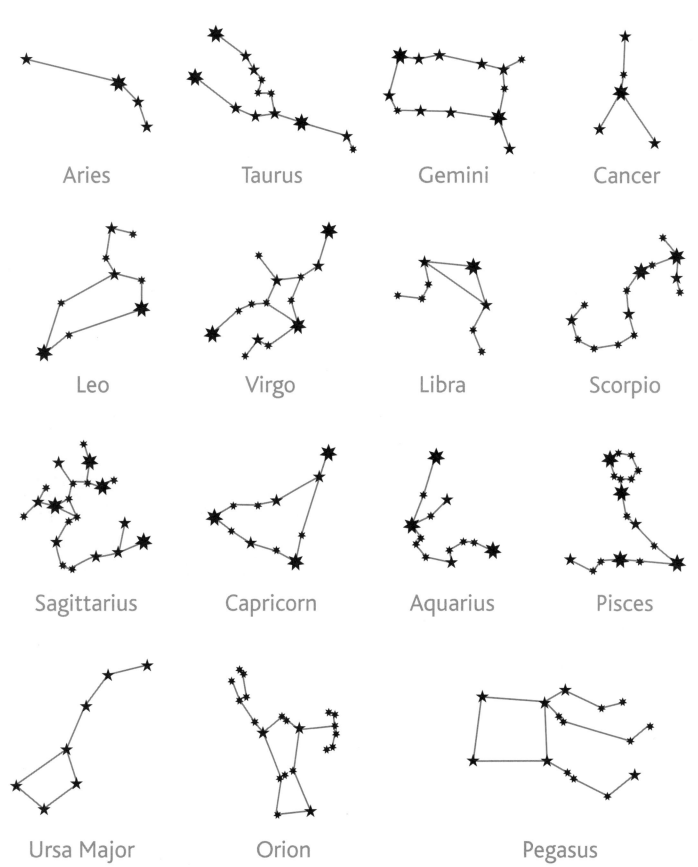

Aries   Taurus   Gemini   Cancer

Leo   Virgo   Libra   Scorpio

Sagittarius   Capricorn   Aquarius   Pisces

Ursa Major   Orion   Pegasus

Can be
done inside

Suitable for
teams

Be extra safety-
conscious

18. MOON PHASES

What are the different phases of the moon?

You will need

- A lamp with a bare light bulb (lampshade removed)
- A small ball (e.g. a ping pong or polystyrene ball)
- A pencil
- Sticky tape
- Moon phases resource (see page 34)
- A camera

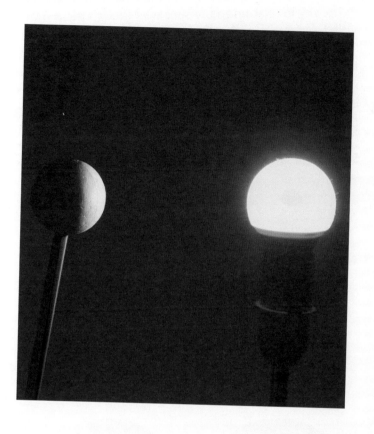

How to do it

Note: You will need adult supervision to make sure you keep a safe distance from the light bulb and avoid tripping over the power cord.

1. Place the ball on the end of the pencil, attaching it with sticky tape. This will represent the moon.

2. Create a dark environment by turning off the main lights. Minimise natural light from the windows by closing the curtains or blinds.

3. Position the lamp on a table, then turn it on. The light bulb will represent the sun. Be careful not to look directly at it as it could hurt your eyes.

4. Face towards the lamp and hold the pencil in one hand, extending your arm forward so that the moon (ball) is level with your forehead.

5. You now represent the earth. Stand in one place and slowly turn around in a full circle (360 degrees), keeping your arm level with your forehead as you do so. If you find that your body is blocking the path of the light to the ball then raise your arm slightly until the ball is fully illuminated. Watch the moon carefully as it 'orbits' the earth. Can you see each of the phases of the moon reflected on the ball? Work with a partner to take a photo of each phase.

Optional: What fraction of the moon appears in each phase? Can you express this as a percentage?

Investigate

Find out what phase the moon is currently in by researching it on the internet or using a night sky app.

What are we learning?

The moon does not emit light. Instead, its surface reflects light from the sun. We can see a different amount of the moon illuminated at different times depending on its position in the sky in relation to the sun. Even though the moon is rotating, only one side is ever visible from the earth. This is called the 'near side'. The 'far side' is never seen from earth. The moon takes 29.5 days to orbit the earth and goes through eight different phases (appearances). These are: new moon, waxing crescent, first quarter, waxing gibbous, full moon, waning gibbous, third quarter, waning crescent. As we see more of the moon, this is called waxing, and then as we see less it is called waning. In the first quarter, 50% of the visible side of the moon's surface is illuminated. It waxes until it becomes a full moon (100% illuminated), then wanes. In the third quarter phase of the lunar cycle, it is back to 50% illumination of the visible side of the moon's surface.

Astronomer

Meteorologist

Moon Phases Resource

New

Waxing crescent

First quarter

Waxing gibbous

Full

Waning gibbous

Third quarter

Waning crescent

Can be
done inside

Can be done
individually

Suitable for
teams

19. MUSICAL INSTRUMENTS

How can we create a range of musical sounds?

You will need

- Recycled materials (e.g. cardboard boxes and tubes, plastic bottles, plastic containers, straws and paper cups)
- Elastic bands
- Lolly sticks
- Balloons
- Beads or dried rice
- Sticky tape
- Scissors

How to do it

1. The challenge is to create a musical instrument (or set of instruments if you are working in a team) that is able to create a range of sounds.

2. Take a look at the materials provided and quickly decide on the kind of instrument you will create. For example, your instrument might have strings like a guitar (elastic bands are good for this) or a skin across the top like a drum (perhaps a balloon stretched across a container or cup).

3. Begin building your instrument.

4. Now practise playing your instrument. Is it easy to use? What limitations does it have? Can you think of a way to adapt it to make it better?

Optional: If you're working in a team, see if you can create a short piece of music to play as a band.

Investigate

Now see if you can modify your musical instrument design to amplify the sound, making it louder. How could you adapt it to make it quieter? How about increasing or decreasing the pitch?

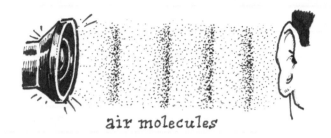

air molecules

What are we learning?

There are lots of types of musical instrument that you can create for this activity. Each instrument creates sound waves, which are temporary compressions in the air. These sounds are made when objects vibrate. With some of your instruments, you may be able to see these vibrations – for example, by plucking a stretched elastic band. These disturbances travel through space and ultimately make your eardrum vibrate, to be heard as sound. Depending on how fast the sound waves vibrate (the frequency) you will hear a different pitch (notes). The sound created by your instruments will also vary in loudness, depending on the materials you have used to build them. The volume is determined by the amplitude (size) of the sound waves.

Product designer

Sound engineer

Can be
done inside

Suitable for
teams

20. NO HANDS PYRAMID

How easy is it to replace human hands in a stacking task?

You will need

- Paper cups
- String
- Elastic bands
- A timer
- A measuring tape

Computer programmer

Robotics engineer

Investigate

See if you can build the same pyramid with all the cups facing upwards instead. Find out more about smart materials.

How to do it

1. You need to create the tallest pyramid that you can out of paper cups. However, there's a catch – you can't touch the cups with your hands or any other body part!

2. Choose which materials you are going to use to help you assemble the pyramid. Consider ways to lift and assemble each cup using these materials. Working as part of a team will be important for this.

3. Start the timer and begin assembling your pyramid. Each cup should be facing downwards.

4. Time is up! Measure your pyramid to see how tall it is. What strategies worked well for construction?

Optional: Now try this activity again but this time you cannot talk to anyone else in your team while you build your pyramid. You will need to think carefully about other ways to communicate!

What are we learning?

A good strategy to help lift the cups is to tie three or four pieces of string to an elastic band, pulling the strings to widen the elastic band and place it around the cup and releasing them to tighten the elastic and capture the cup. This method is reliant on good teamwork. All group members must communicate well and coordinate their efforts. Working well in a team is important in all STEM careers. For example, engineers often solve tricky problems by working together.

The manual job of picking up cups can be replaced by a robotic arm. Robotic arms can be found on factory production lines and are controlled by computers. Increasingly, roboticists are considering using innovative soft materials ('soft robotics') for grippers at the end of the arms. 'Smart' materials include shape-memory polymers (SMPs) that can temporarily deform and then return to their original shape. This change can be in response to an electrical current, for example.

Can be done inside   Can be done individually

21. OCEAN PLASTIC PROBLEM

How does plastic in the ocean affect marine animals?

You will need

- A tray
- Frozen sweetcorn and peas
- Small bits of plastic (e.g. sweet wrappers) or recyclable plastic
- Tweezers, chopsticks or another picking tool

How to do it

1. Fill up a tray with water: this will represent the ocean.

2. Scatter frozen sweetcorn and peas in the water to represent the food that marine animals might eat (some will sink and some will float).

3. Add small bits of plastic (e.g. sweet wrappers) to the water to represent some of the plastic obstacles that marine animals might encounter.

4. Imagine that you are a sea bird, looking for food. How much can you collect using your beak (represented by your tools of choice)? Be careful to avoid the plastic!

Investigate

What plants and animals are most affected by plastic in the ocean? Can you find some ways to minimise plastic waste?

What are we learning?

Marine plastic pollution is caused when plastic from the land ends up in the sea. This is dangerous to many marine animals as it can lead to ingestion (swallowing), suffocation (restricted breathing) or entanglement (being tangled up). Tiny pieces of plastic are called microplastics. These often result from larger pieces of plastic breaking down into tiny pieces. As marine animals travel through the ocean in search of food they risk ingesting these microplastics. The toxic chemicals within them can cause animals to become unwell. They may even reach the human food chain and water supply. By disposing of plastic carefully, including by using recycling facilities, we can help to prevent this.

Environmental scientist

Marine biologist

Can be
done inside

Can be done
individually

Suitable for
teams

22. ORIGAMI ENGINEERING

How are the principles of
origami applied to engineering?

You will need

- A4 paper
- Sticky tape
- A ruler
- Toy cars
- Two tables or chairs

Investigate

NASA have recently designed a device
called a 'starshade' which can shield a
telescope's camera from the bright light
of other stars so it can take detailed
pictures. Find out about how origami
was influential in the design.

How to do it

1. The challenge is to create the strongest bridge you can using just one piece of paper.

2. Begin by laying a length of A4 paper across a 25-centimetre gap between two raised surfaces (e.g. two tables or chairs). Tape the paper to either side of the raised surface using a single piece of sticky tape at each end.

3. Test the strength of the paper bridge by placing toy cars onto it, one at a time. How many can it hold before it collapses?

4. Start again with a new piece of A4 paper and see if you can improve the strength of your bridge by folding the paper. You could choose to use one of the origami folds pictured or you could create your own. Remember, you can only use one piece of paper.

5. Test the strength of each design by taping it down in the same way and placing toy cars onto the bridge until it collapses. Which paper fold was the strongest?

mountain fold

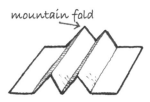

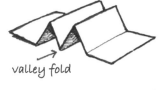

valley fold

What are we learning?

The ancient Japanese art of origami (paper folding) has many real-world applications in engineering. Origami principles help fit large objects into a smaller shape which can be unfolded quickly when needed. For example, engineers took inspiration from origami patterns and folding methods to design the way in which car airbags are stored and deployed. Many space projects have used folding principles from origami – for example, the solar arrays (panels) which generate electricity for the International Space Station. You probably found that the strongest bridge involved layering the paper to reinforce it. Building materials are often reinforced (made of different layers) to add extra strength.

Civil
engineer

Mathematician

Can be
done inside

Can be done
individually

Suitable for
teams

23. PAPER CHAIN CHALLENGE

What's the longest paper chain you can create using only one piece of A4 paper?

You will need

- A4 paper
- Scissors
- Sticky tape
- A tape measure
- Something to use as a weight (e.g. toy car)

Investigate

Repeat the activity but this time try to create the strongest chain you can using only one piece of paper. Test how strong it is by holding it in the air and hanging a weight (e.g. a toy car) from the bottom link of the chain.

How to do it

1. Using one piece of A4 paper, some sticky tape and a pair of scissors, your challenge is to create the longest paper chain you can!

2. Cut your paper into strips. You will need to decide whether you think it will be best to cut your paper vertically or horizontally. You will also need to decide on the optimum width of the strips.

3. Once you have cut your paper into strips, begin to assemble it into a paper chain. To do this, loop the ends of the first strip of paper together and tape them up to create a paper ring. Then thread the second strip of paper through the ring and tape the ends together to create two adjoining rings. Continue until all the strips have been added.

4. Once your chain is complete, lay it out in a straight line across a flat surface, pulling it taut to make it as long as you can (without breaking it!). Measure from one end to the other with a tape measure. How long is your paper chain? How could you improve your design to make it even longer?

What are we learning?

You should have found that the longest chain consists of narrow strips of paper, cut vertically. If you were to make the strongest chain, a good technique would be to increase the width of each strip or to increase the thickness of each ring by folding the paper strips before sticking the ends together. In real-life we see chains used for a variety of reasons, including decoration (e.g. in bracelets or necklaces), transferring power (e.g. a bike chain), security and protection (e.g. a door chain or chain mail armour) or for pulling (e.g. the chain on an anchor or old-fashioned toilet flush). Each chain varies in link length and material depending on its use.

Mathematician

Product
designer

Can be done inside

Can be done individually

Suitable for teams

24. PASTA SKELETONS

What does a human skeleton look like?

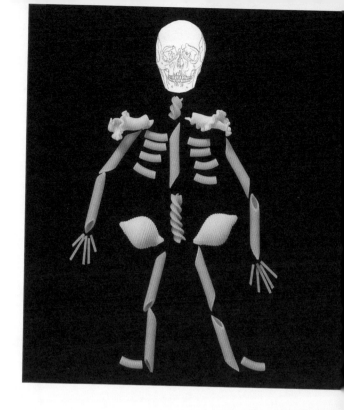

You will need

- A selection of different types of dried pasta (including spaghetti)
- Large piece of paper
- A pencil or pen
- Skeleton resource (see page 42)
- A timer

Investigate

Choose another vertebrate (animal with a backbone) (e.g. a dog) and find out what its skeleton looks like. Can you create it out of pasta? How does it differ from a human skeleton?

What are we learning?

The human skeleton contains around 300 bones at birth. Over time these bones fuse (join) together to create 206 bones by adulthood. While you will not have been able to represent all of these bones, you should have been able to create the overall skeleton structure, including the vertebrae (a series of small bones forming the backbone), the rib cage, the pelvis, the three arm bones (humerus, radius and ulna) and the four leg bones (femur, patella, tibia and fibula). Forensic scientists are able to analyse human bones to find out information about the person, including their age, gender and race.

How to do it

Note: The human skeleton is made up of lots of different bones, so it would be extremely difficult to represent them all! Instead, focus on creating the overall structure.

1. The challenge is to create the most accurate skeleton you can in just 15 minutes using pasta to represent the different bones.

2. Before you begin, draw the skull at the top of a large piece of paper.

3. Start the timer and begin to construct the rest of the skeleton. **Hint:** Start at the top and work downwards.

4. Look carefully at your skeleton and think about whether you have missed any important bones. Leave a gap between your pasta bones to represent the joints. Remember to use longer pieces of spaghetti to represent long bones and to snap your pasta or spaghetti pieces to represent smaller bones. If you find there is a bone that you cannot represent with pasta, you could always draw it instead.

5. Time is up! Step back and compare your skeleton to the skeleton resource. Which bones have you included? Which did you forget?

Optional: Younger children may find it helpful to take a quick look at the skeleton resource before they begin the activity, or to have a copy in front of them throughout the task.

Doctor

Forensic scientist

Skeleton Resource

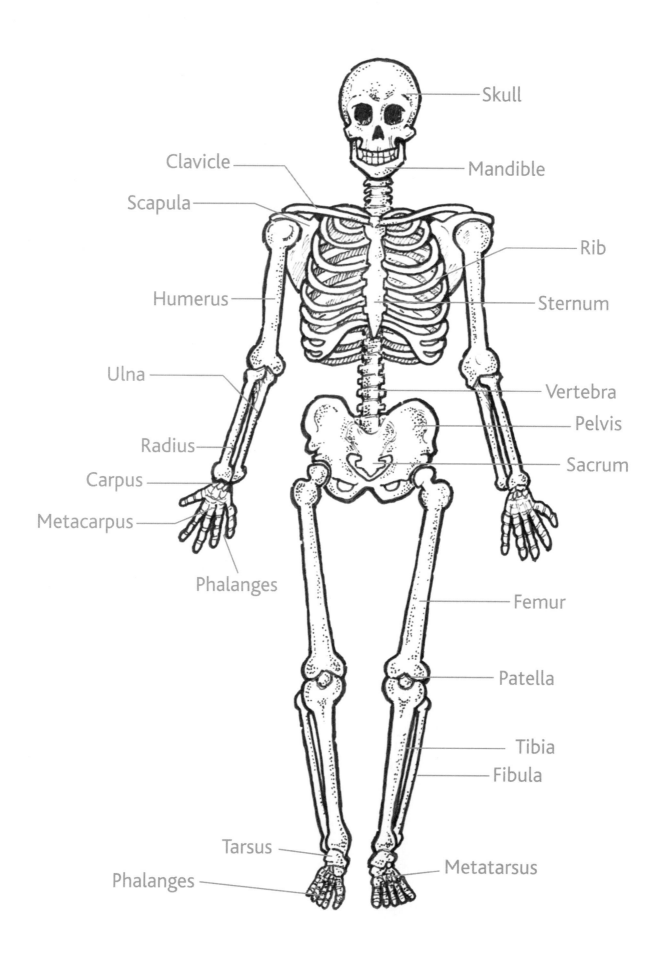

Skull

Clavicle

Scapula

Mandible

Rib

Sternum

Humerus

Ulna

Vertebra

Pelvis

Radius

Sacrum

Carpus

Metacarpus

Phalanges

Femur

Patella

Tibia

Fibula

Tarsus

Metatarsus

Phalanges

Can be done inside

Can be done individually

25. PEEPING PERISCOPES

How can we see over something taller than us without standing on tiptoes?

You will need

- Paper or card
- Scissors
- Periscope template (see page 44)
- Small plastic craft mirrors x2
- Sticky tape or glue

Physicist

Sailor

Investigate

Does the periscope work if the mirrors are at an angle other than 45°? Can you explain why this is?

What are we learning?

Periscopes allow us to see over walls and around corners. This is due to the way that light is reflected off the mirrors inside the periscope. Light hits the top mirror and is reflected down the periscope tube. The law of reflection states that the angle of incidence (the angle of the light going into the mirror) equals the angle of reflection (the light coming out). For the periscope to work the mirrors must be placed parallel to each other at an angle of 45° to the incident light. Submarines use periscopes to help the crew see what is above the surface of the water. Periscopes are also used by tanks and armoured vehicles to allow the occupants to inspect the area around them without leaving the safety of the vehicle.

How to do it

1. Photocopy or trace a copy of the periscope template resource. Cut around the solid lines of the periscope template. Then fold along the dotted lines and use glue or sticky tape to assemble the periscope structure.

2. Loosely attach a mirror at either end using a single piece of sticky tape. **Note:** You may need to trim your mirrors down to size.

3. Bend the flaps of the periscope until you find an angle that allows the reflection in the top mirror to also be visible in the bottom mirror. Then firmly tape the mirrors in place. **Hint:** The mirrors need to be parallel to each other at a 45° angle.

4. Hold the periscope so the top end pokes out above the top of a wall and look at the bottom mirror. Can you see over the wall?

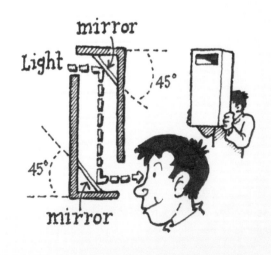

Periscope Template

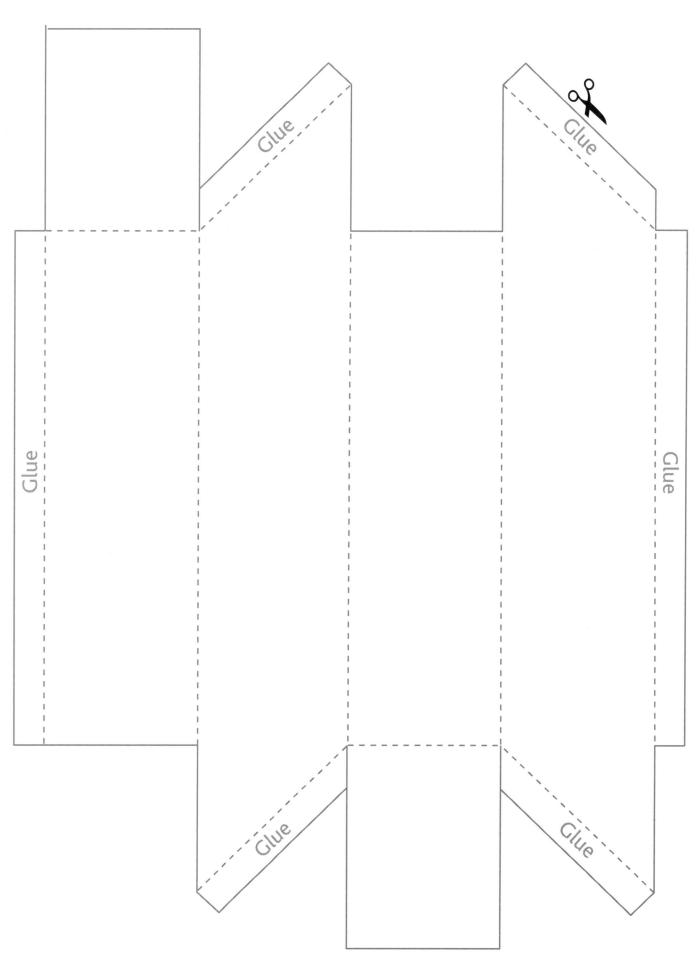

Can be done inside

Can be done individually

Suitable for teams

26. PIRATE SHIP PLANK

What is the purpose of a cantilever?

You will need

- 30-centimetre rulers or 30-centimetre strips of thick cardboard x3 (minimum)
- Coins
- A table
- A measuring tape
- A timer

Civil engineer

Sailor

Investigate

Research some famous examples of cantilevers (e.g. the Forth Bridge in Scotland or Frank Lloyd Wright's Fallingwater house in the USA).

How to do it

1. Your challenge is to create the longest plank you can, cantilevered (projected) off the edge of a pirate ship (a table).

2. Start the 15-minute timer. Then begin by taking the first plank (ruler or piece of cardboard) and anchoring it onto the edge of the ship, with part of it projecting outwards. Use the coins to weight the plank in place. Think carefully about how many coins you need to use and where they should be positioned on the plank.

3. Continue to extend the plank outwards over the 'sea' by adding extra rulers or pieces of cardboard, using coins to hold them in place. Each time you extend the plank you will need to think about where you position the coins in order to keep the plank projected off the side of the ship.

4. When the time is up, use a measuring tape to measure the length of your plank. What strategies were most successful in creating it?

What are we learning?

A pirate ship plank is an example of a cantilever. A cantilever is a beam that is only attached on one end. Most beams are attached at both ends. Examples of cantilevers used in engineering include cantilever bridges, cantilever balconies and cantilever cranes. To successfully create your pirate ship plank, you will need to place enough coins on the part of the plank that rests on the ship (table). This helps to support the weight overhanging the ship. If you place too many coins on the cantilevered plank, it will topple into the sea!

Can be done inside

Can be done individually

Suitable for teams

27. PULLEY FLAGPOLES

How can pulley systems help us?

You will need

- A wooden dowel or stick (approximately 30 centimetres in length)
- Plasticine
- String
- Bulldog clips x2
- Paper
- Colouring pencils or felt-tip pens
- Scissors
- Sticky tape

Mechanical engineer

Sailor

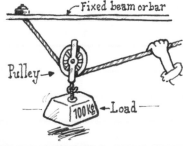

Investigate

A moveable pulley allows you to use less force to lift a load. Find some examples of how moveable pulleys are used.

What are we learning?

Flagpoles are typically made of wood or metal. They are often too tall for a person to be able to reach the flag, so a pulley system is used to raise and lower it. A pulley is a simple device for lifting things. In this activity we have created a fixed pulley system by looping string between the bulldog clips on our flagpole. This means that the pulley stays in one place, allowing us to lift an object by pulling on the rope. The rope on a real flagpole is called a halyard. Other uses of pulley systems include to hoist a sail on a boat or to extend a ladder.

How to do it

1. Begin by cutting out a paper rectangle: 10 centimetres by 5 centimetres is a good size. Then decorate it to create a flag. You can choose whether to replicate a world flag or design your own.

2. Create a flagpole by placing a wooden dowel or stick into a lump of plasticine so that it stands up vertically.

3. Take two bulldog clips and attach them to the top and bottom of your flagpole. Adjust their positioning so that the arms of both the clips are sticking out in the same direction.

4. Take a long piece of string (roughly double the length of your flagpole) and thread one of the ends through the holes in the clips. Loop it back and tie the string so that it creates a tight loop. Then cut off any excess string.

5. Wrap the end of your flag around the flagpole string and use sticky tape to secure it in place. Make sure you stick the tape to the paper flag and not directly onto the string.

6. Gently pull the string to raise and lower your flag!

Best done outside

Can be done individually

Suitable for teams

28. RAINBOW LEAF WALK

Why do leaves change colour?

You will need

- Leaves
- A nature book or the LeafSnap app (or similar app)

Investigate

Choose your favourite leaf from your collection and find out what type of tree it comes from. You could use a nature book to identify it, or photograph the leaf against a white background using the LeafSnap app, which will identify the species for you. Why are some trees 'evergreen'?

How to do it

Note: Autumn is the best time of year for this activity.

1. Begin by going on a nature walk to collect different coloured leaves. The aim is to find a leaf to represent every colour of the rainbow. Remember to only collect leaves that have fallen on the ground.

2. Once you have a good collection of leaves, sort them into the different colours. Check you have a good representation of each colour before creating your rainbow.

3. To create a rainbow the coloured leaves should be arranged in order: red, orange, yellow, green, blue and purple (indigo and violet).

4. After arranging your leaves, discuss what you have found. Which colours were easiest to find? Were there any colours that you couldn't find?

Optional: Add a further challenge by making sure that each leaf is a different size or shape.

What are we learning?

The colour of a leaf comes down to an important biological pigment called chlorophyll. A pigment is a substance that absorbs particular parts of the light spectrum. Chlorophyll absorbs mostly blue and some red light, reflecting back the bright green colour that we see. Put simply, chlorophyll is the substance that allows plants to absorb the blue and red light energy from the sun and turn it into food. This process is called photosynthesis. Because of the presence of chlorophyll, the leaves of most plants are green. As the sunlight diminishes and the temperature drops in the autumn, this food-making process slows and stops. The chlorophyll breaks down and the green colour disappears. Acting with other chemical changes, this causes some leaves to turn shades of autumnal red, purple and yellow. The lack of sunlight and food eventually causes the leaves to turn brown. There is no true blue pigment in plants, so it's rare to see blue leaves.

Botanist

Dendrologist

Can be
done inside

Suitable for
teams

29. RAMP RACING

How can we make best use of gravity to speed a car along?

You will need

- Large pieces of cardboard
- A toy car
- A range of different textured materials (paper, tinfoil, a rug, bubble wrap, sandpaper, etc.)
- Scissors
- Glue or sticky tape
- A measuring tape
- A timer
- A table or chair
- Pencil and paper (optional)

Investigate

Now adapt your ramp to make your car travel the shortest distance possible. What materials might you use for this? Find out about car tyre tread designs and what snow tyres look like.

How to do it

Note: Bear in mind that the outcome of this activity will differ depending on variables such as the height of the top of the ramp and the surface of the floor underneath the ramp.

1. The challenge is to create a ramp, in just 15 minutes, that will enable a toy car to travel the furthest distance.

2. Cut a rectangle out of a large piece of cardboard (it's up to you how long it is) to make your ramp. Then suspend it from the edge of a raised surface (e.g. a table or chair) onto the floor. The height of the ramp is your choice.

3. Position the measuring tape along the floor in the direction of travel, lining the start of the tape up with the bottom of the ramp. Then test your ramp to see how far the toy car travels, checking the distance using the measuring tape. You may need to adjust the angle or length of the ramp to vary the distance.

4. Now see if you can increase the distance that the car travels by adding different materials to the surface of the ramp. Write down the distance using a pencil and paper (optional).

5. When the time is up, reflect on which adaptation of the ramp allowed the car to travel the furthest. How could you improve your ramp design?

What are we learning?

Gravity is the force that pulls the toy car to the ground. As the wheels make contact with the cardboard ramp they create an opposing force called friction. This slows the car down. Smoother surfaces like shiny tinfoil create less friction, allowing the car to travel faster and further. Rougher surfaces like a rug or sandpaper create greater friction, slowing the speed and reducing the distance of travel. A real car needs some friction, though, in order for its wheels to grip the road: think of a car skidding on ice. The angle of the incline also affects the speed of travel: the steeper the incline, the faster the car travels. Mechanical engineers take these factors into consideration when designing ramps for daily use. For example, wheelchair ramps have gradual inclines and are covered in a material that creates friction, making them safer to use. Skateboarding ramps often have smoother surfaces and steeper inclines to increase speed.

Mechanical engineer

Physicist

Can be done inside

Suitable for teams

30. RUBE GOLDBERG MACHINES

How could you design a machine to perform a simple activity?

You will need

- A marble
- A cup
- A range of materials (e.g. building blocks, cardboard tubes, dominoes, string, sticky tack)
- A timer

What are we learning?

Rube Goldberg was an American cartoonist and engineer who imagined complicated machines to carry out very simple tasks. Each machine consisted of a variety of different sections that joined together to create a chain reaction to achieve the final goal. Not only are his designs funny, they showcase a variety of examples of engineering – including pulley systems, levers, pendulums and gears. In reality, engineers try to find the simplest and most reliable way to carry out tasks when they are designing machines. Heath Robinson was a British cartoonist who also imagined fantastical machines. People use the term 'Heath Robinson' to describe complex, impractical devices or schemes.

How to do it

Note: It will be helpful to look at a few examples of Rube Goldberg machines before you begin this activity. You can find lots on the Rube Goldberg website: https://www.rubegoldberg.com/.

1. The challenge is to create a machine to roll a marble into a cup that's placed on its side. However, this is a Rube Goldberg machine so it should be complex!

2. Before you begin, look at the materials available and quickly decide on the design of your machine. Think about the machine construction as a series of steps. Start the timer.

3. Start with the final step: find a way to roll the marble into the cup (e.g. by knocking over a line of dominoes that nudge the marble, pushing it into the cup).

4. Add additional steps onto your machine, working backwards.

5. Time is up! Test your machine to see if it works.

Investigate

Now see if you can create a machine that takes exactly 30 seconds to complete the task of knocking the marble into the cup.

Mechanical engineer

Physicist

Best done
outside

Can be done
individually

Be extra safety-
conscious

31. SALT PENDULUM

What patterns can we see in a pendulum swing?

You will need

- Fine salt (or sand)
- Food colouring (optional)
- A bowl
- A plastic or paper cup
- String
- A sharp pencil
- Plastic sheeting or a tray (optional)

Investigate

Now try attaching the string to the branch in two places, joining it in the middle at a single point. How does this change the salt pattern? What happens to the pattern if you change the spacing of the two pieces of string on the branch?

How to do it

Note: Prepare for this activity in advance by mixing the salt with a few drops of food colouring in a bowl, allowing it time to dry (optional). You may need adult support to pierce the holes in the cup.

1. Take your plastic cup and punch four evenly spaced holes around the edges of the top of the cup.

2. Find something to tie the string of your pendulum onto (e.g. a low hanging branch or monkey bars). Tie a long piece of string around it, leaving one end hanging downwards. Then attach your cup to it by threading four shorter pieces of string of equal length through each of the holes and tying them to the longer piece of string.

3. Place plastic sheeting or a tray underneath the cup to catch the salt (unless you are working on a surface that can be swept clean afterwards).

4. Pierce a small hole (about 3 millimetres wide) in the bottom of the cup for the salt to escape through using a sharp pencil. Then place your finger over the hole as you tip the salt into the cup.

5. Remove your finger, swing the cup in a straight line and watch the pattern the salt creates on the surface below.

6. Now swing the cup with a circular motion.

What are we learning?

A pendulum is a weight suspended from a pivot that can swing freely. In this case, the weight is the cup full of salt and the pivot is the branch. When displaced (moved) from its equilibrium (resting) position, the pendulum (cup) oscillates (swings from side to side). This is due to the downward force of gravity: as the weight swings up against gravity, potential (stored) energy increases, and as it swings back again this potential energy changes to kinetic (movement) energy. Frictional forces (from the air, and between attachment points) mean the amplitude (size) of the swings decline over time until the pendulum eventually stops. Importantly, the weight of a pendulum does not affect its period (the time it takes to swing back and forth once). If you give a circular swing to the pendulum it will trace out an elliptical (oval) shape that steadily reduces in size as the swing declines. The pattern traced out is called a Lissajous curve.

Mathematician

Physicist

Can be
done inside

Can be done
individually

Suitable for
teams

32. SCARED PEPPER

What is surface tension?

You will need

- A shallow bowl
- Ground pepper
- Water
- Washing-up liquid
- Milk and salt (optional)

How to do it

1. Half-fill a shallow bowl with room-temperature water.

2. Sprinkle a layer of pepper onto the water. Then stick your finger into the water in the centre of the bowl and observe what happens.

3. Add a squirt of washing-up liquid to the tip of your finger and insert it again into the centre of the bowl. What happens this time? How is it different to the previous reaction?

Investigate

Explore what happens if you use milk instead of water. Explore what happens if you use salt instead of pepper. Read about water strider insects that can walk on water.

What are we learning?

The water in the bowl has a high surface tension, creating a kind of 'skin' on the surface. Surface tension exists because water molecules cling together tightly (cohesive force), and at the interface between the water and the air this cohesive force is stronger than the adhesive force to the neighbouring air molecules, pulling the water molecules inwards. The grains of pepper don't dissolve in water and are so light they don't break the surface tension of the water, causing them to float on the top. The washing-up liquid reduces the surface tension. It breaks the tight skin on the water, a bit like popping a balloon. This water surface is suddenly able to pull away from your finger, which pulls the pepper with it.

Some birds (e.g. ducks) use their feathers to stay dry. One of the reasons why feathers keep off water is because they are coated in a special biological oil. They are hydrophobic, meaning they can repel water. If birds get cleaning products on their feathers, they can become waterlogged. This is another reason to dispose of cleaning products carefully.

Chemist

Marine
biologist

Return to activity later

Best done outside

Can be done individually

33. SHADOWS AND SUNDIALS

How did people tell the time before clocks?

You will need

- Flat rocks x12
- Paint and a paintbrush or marker pens
- A stick (approximately 30 centimetres in length)
- A watch or clock
- Plasticine (optional)

Investigate

Come back to your sundial the following day. See if you can tell the time accurately when it's not exactly on the hour. You may need to use your knowledge of fractions to help you.

How to do it

Note: You will need to do this activity on a sunny day. You will need to return to it throughout the day. If you are doing this activity at school, you will only be able to add the rocks for the hours that fall within the school day.

1. Begin the activity first thing in the morning by collecting 12 rocks and a stick. Try to choose rocks with a flat surface as you will need to write a number on each of them.

2. Use paint or marker pens to number each of the rocks from 1 to 12. Each of these rocks will represent an hour on the 12-hour clock.

3. Find an open space in full sunlight and place the stick in the ground so that it stands up vertically. Use plasticine to hold the stick in place if the surface is paved or tarmacked. On the hour, take note of where the shadow falls and place the rock with the number corresponding to the current hour in the path of the shadow.

4. Return each hour, on the hour, to check the position of the stick's shadow, adding the corresponding numbered rock to create the dial of the 12-hour clock.

What are we learning?

A sundial is a device that uses the sun to tell the time. The part of a sundial that casts a shadow (our stick) is called a gnomon (pronounced 'no-mon'). Sundials have been used by many civilisations throughout history. For example, one of the world's oldest sundials, dating to around 1300 BC, was found in Egypt's Valley of the Kings.

Light travels in a straight line. When we place our gnomon – in this case a stick – in its path it blocks some of the light, creating a shadow. As the earth rotates, the position of the sun in the sky changes, which changes the length and position of shadows. In the morning, the sun rises in the east, and the shadow is longer and cast west. By midday, the sun is directly overhead, making the shadow short. In the afternoon, the sun is setting in the west and the shadow grows longer and is cast east.

Astronomer

Meteorologist

Best done
outside

Suitable for
teams

34. SPIDERWEB ENGINEERING

How easy is it to make a good spiderweb?

You will need

- A hula hoop
- String or wool
- Scissors
- Small balls (e.g. tennis balls)
- A timer
- Sticks (optional)
- Spray bottle and water (optional)

Investigate

Take a closer look at the architecture of spiderwebs in the natural environment. Spray a fine mist of water using a clean spray bottle to make the web's fine details stand out (this will not harm the web).

How to do it

1. You will have just 15 minutes to create a 'spiderweb' (using string) within the hula hoop that will be able to hold 'prey' (small balls). The success of the activity will be defined by how much prey the web can capture without it falling through onto the ground below.

2. Start the timer and begin to create your web by threading wool or string onto the hoop. **Hint:** Tie the thread across your hoop as though you are creating bicycle spokes. Then create circles within your hoop by wrapping the thread around the spokes. (See activity 17 for knot suggestions to help you tie the string.)

3. Time is up! Hold your web out horizontally and ask a partner to stand two steps back from the web and gently throw the prey into the middle. How many items of prey can your web hold? How could you improve your web so it could hold more prey?

Optional: Instead of using a hula hoop, try creating the frame using natural materials such as sticks.

What are we learning?

Spiders often use webs to catch prey for food. A classic orb web is shaped like a bicycle wheel, perhaps like the web you have created. Unlike yours, each web takes about two hours to complete and is made of spider silk, spun from spinnerets on the spider's abdomen. Spider silk has a high tensile strength (can withstand a high tension), so it does not break apart when a heavy weight is applied to it. Weight for weight, spider silk is stronger than steel. It also has good extensibility, meaning it is able to stretch a long way without breaking. Because of these properties, humans are interested in creating artificial spider silk to use in clothing, military body armour and parachute material, and for repairing ligaments (the connective tissue between bones).

Aerospace engineer

Entomologist

Can be
done inside

Can be done
individually

Suitable for
teams

35. STRAW ROLLER COASTERS

How do roller coasters work?

You will need

- A cardboard box (shoebox size or bigger)
- Straws
- Plasticine
- Scissors
- A ping pong ball

Investigate

Find out more about what g-force is and how it is used in different theme park rides.

How to do it

1. Before you begin, quickly decide on a building strategy for your roller coaster. You will need to give particular thought to the height and the shape.

2. Turn the cardboard box upside down to create a flat base and position your first two straws on the base. Secure them in place with a lump of plasticine so that they stand up vertically, checking that they are approximately the same distance apart as the width of the ping pong ball. They will form the first two – and the highest – 'legs' of your roller coaster frame.

3. Trim the next set of legs so they are shorter than the first. This will create a slight incline to the 'track' for the ball to roll down. Add the first two pieces of track (straws) to the top of these legs, attaching them with more plasticine. The two straws should be placed parallel to each other with enough space between them for the ping pong ball to roll along.

4. Continue to add more legs and track to your roller coaster, working downwards towards the base. Your roller coaster will be complete when it can carry the ping pong ball from the top of the frame all the way to the base.

What are we learning?

Before the ball travels down the roller coaster track, it has potential energy after being raised up against the force of gravity. As it begins to move, this converts into kinetic (movement) energy. Some of the energy of the ball is lost to friction as it travels down the track. Well-designed straw roller coasters allow the ball to complete the entire course without coming to a stop along the way. In a real roller coaster, a series of gears and chains pull the car to the top. Roller coasters create a thrill by inducing stomach-leaping accelerations on passengers in the car: up and down and side to side. These accelerations can be described in units of gravitational force equivalent, or g-force, to create perceptions of weight (think of the sensation of being heavily pinned into your roller coaster seat).

Mechanical
engineer

Physicist

Can be done inside

Can be done individually

36. TANTALISING TANGRAMS

How can geometric shapes be rearranged to form new patterns?

You will need

- Tangram template (see page 56) (copied onto card)
- Scissors
- A timer

How to do it

1. Take the tangram template and cut it out along the solid lines into the seven individual pieces.

2. The challenge is to create each of the pictures shown below the tangram template using all seven tangram pieces. To make it harder, the pictures are coloured solid black so you can't see the individual shape outlines. How many can you complete in just 15 minutes?

3. Time is up! Did you manage to recreate the pictures? Take a look in the back of the book (see page 67) to find the answers to each.

Optional: Create another picture of your choice (e.g. a person or an animal) using all seven pieces.

Investigate

What geometrical shapes can you create using all seven pieces? For example, try a square, rectangle, triangle or parallelogram.

What are we learning?

Tangrams originated in medieval China. They are 'dissection' puzzles, consisting of seven 2D shapes, arranged into the starting shape of a square. The seven shapes consist of two large triangles, two medium triangles, two small triangles, one square and one parallelogram. The individual pieces can be rearranged together to make thousands of other shapes, a bit like a reverse jigsaw. For example, you will have tried to arrange them into the shape of a boat, a house and a bridge. Tangrams help to develop important skills such as spatial awareness and visualisation. These are skills that architects use frequently when imagining how objects will fit into a space.

Architect

Mathematician

Tangram Template

Resource from *15-Minute STEM Book 2* © Emily Hunt, 2020
Available to download from www.crownhouse.co.uk/featured/15-minute-stem-2

Best done outside

Can be done individually

Suitable for teams

37. VOLCANIC ERUPTIONS

Why do volcanoes erupt?

You will need

- A plastic bottle (or glass jar)
- Vinegar
- Bicarbonate of soda
- Red food colouring
- Newspaper
- Cardboard
- Scissors
- Sticky tape
- A dessertspoon
- Decorating materials (e.g. brown paper)

How to do it

1. Begin by cutting a square base for the volcano out of cardboard. Then position the plastic bottle vertically in the middle of the base and remove the lid. The top of the bottle will form the volcano crater.

2. Build up the shape of the volcano by scrunching up newspaper and layering it around the outside of the bottle. Use sticky tape to hold it in place.

3. When you are happy with the shape of the volcano, decorate it (e.g. by wrapping brown paper over the newspaper).

4. Place a couple of dessertspoonfuls of bicarbonate of soda inside the plastic bottle. Then add some drops of red food colouring.

5. Carefully tip in the vinegar, stopping when you can see the liquid inside bubbling to the top of the plastic bottle. Stand back and watch the volcano erupt!

Investigate

There are two main types of volcano: composite and shield. Find out more about their similarities and differences.

What are we learning?

The acid in the vinegar reacts with the bicarbonate of soda, creating bubbles of carbon dioxide. These gas bubbles rise to the surface, giving the same visual effect as in a volcanic eruption. This is a chemical reaction. In real life, volcanoes are openings in the earth's surface. They can often be found at the meeting points between tectonic plates (pieces of the earth's surface that fit together like a jigsaw puzzle). In an eruption, red hot magma from beneath the earth's crust is pushed up to the surface and escapes through the volcano. Once the magma erupts it is called lava. These eruptions can be incredibly dangerous to anyone near the volcano. Geologists classify volcanoes by the frequency of their eruptions: active volcanoes have recently erupted or will erupt soon; dormant volcanoes have not erupted for a long time but could erupt in future; extinct volcanoes have no possibility of eruption.

Chemist

Geologist

Can be done inside

Can be done individually

38. WATER BOTTLE FOUNTAIN

How can we help people access drinking water?

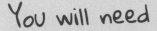

You will need

- A plastic bottle
- A bendable straw
- A pair of scissors
- Sticky tack or plasticine
- A balloon
- A jug of water
- A bowl or tray
- A clothes peg (optional)

Investigate

Experiment with different amounts of water in the bottle. What starting level is most effective for the fountain to work?

How to do it

1. Use the scissors to cut a small hole about halfway up the side of the plastic bottle.

2. Insert the straw through the hole so that the long part is pointing down into the bottom of the bottle and the shorter part, and the bendable section, is sticking out of the bottle. Secure it in place on the side of the bottle using sticky tack or plasticine.

3. Pour water into the bottle until it is about two thirds full.

4. Position an empty bowl or tray underneath the sticking-out straw.

5. Blow up the balloon and carefully attach the opening over the top of the bottle. Then watch your water pump dispense water!

Optional: Use a clothes peg on the straw to stop and start the flow of water.

What are we learning?

When we blow into the balloon, we fill it up with pressured air. When this is placed over the bottle, the pressured air pushes down on the water, which then is forced out of the straw. Drinking water fountains are used throughout the world to provide people with access to clean, safe drinking water. Note, however, that in real life water is not pushed out like this. Usually, the water pressure in the mains supply results from gravity. The water source, such as a reservoir or water tower, is higher up and the weight of the water creates pressure in the pipes lower down. Another way of accessing water commonly used in developing countries is a hand pump. When the piston (handle) is pulled upwards, suction brings water from below the ground into the pump head. When the piston is pulled downwards, the valve on the piston opens up and allows water to flow out.

Environmental scientist

Water engineer

Can be done inside

Can be done individually

Suitable for teams

39. WIND TURBINE CHALLENGE

How can we use wind to create useful power?

You will need

- A sharp pencil
- Cardboard
- A hairdryer
- A paper cup
- A table
- Sticky tape
- String
- Scissors

Investigate

Experiment with the blades of your wind turbine, changing elements such as their size, thickness and shape. How does this affect the effectiveness of the wind turbine?

How to do it

Note: You may need adult supervision when using the hairdryer.

1. Position the pencil so that half of it is hanging over the edge of the table – the sharpened end needs to be facing out. This will form the shaft of the wind turbine.

2. Attach the pencil to the table by cutting out two small cardboard rectangles and placing them across the pencil, taping the cardboard rectangles onto the table at each end. They should hold the pencil in place but be attached loosely enough to allow it to rotate.

3. Cut two more rectangles out of cardboard to form the blades of the wind turbine. Attach them by piercing a hole through the middle of each using the sharp end of the pencil and pushing them onto the shaft.

4. Cut a piece of string to approximately 30 centimetres long. Tie one end to the shaft of the pencil and the other to a paper cup.

5. Turn on the hairdryer and position it so that the air turns the blades of the wind turbine. As it does, you should see the pencil rotate, coiling the string around it and pulling up the paper cup.

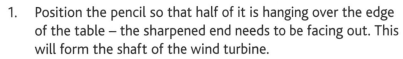

What are we learning?

Throughout history we have harnessed wind power for a variety of uses – for example, propelling sailboats and grinding grain in a windmill. Nowadays, we typically convert it into electricity first. Wind turbines transform the wind's kinetic (movement) energy into electrical energy. The large blades of a wind turbine are caught by the wind and forced to turn, driving a generator either directly (a direct drive turbine) or through a series of gears which speed up the rotation. The stronger the wind, the more electricity is produced. Wind power is a form of renewable energy. This means that the energy collected comes from natural sources and will not run out. Other sources of renewable energy include sunlight (solar energy), flowing rivers (often using dams) and tides (rising and falling sea levels).

Environmental scientist

Meteorologist

40. WINTER COATS

How can you stop ice cubes melting?

You will need

- Ice cubes
- A variety of materials (e.g. tissue paper, bubble wrap, tinfoil, fabric, a plastic bag, polystyrene packaging)
- Elastic bands
- A timer
- A camera (optional)

Investigate

Now see if you can improve your design by combining multiple materials to make an even better insulating coat for the ice cube.

How to do it

1. The challenge is to design the best winter coat to prevent the ice cubes from melting.

2. Wrap each ice cube in a different material. Try not to hold the ice cubes for too long while doing this as it may cause them to melt. Use elastic bands to secure the materials around the ice cubes. These materials represent each of the winter coats.

3. Leave your ice cubes out at room temperature on the same surface and set a timer for ten minutes.

4. When the timer finishes, unwrap each ice cube. Which winter coats have best insulated the ice cubes? Which have been ineffective, with the most melting?

Optional: Take a photo of each ice cube at the start and end of the experiment to see how it has changed.

What are we learning?

Heat transfer can occur between two objects of different temperatures. Thermal energy (heat) is transferred from the hotter object to the colder object until they are the same temperature. A winter coat is an example of a thermal insulator. This means that it greatly reduces heat transfer, acting as a barrier: keeping hot things hot and cold things cold. If we left our ice cubes unwrapped at room temperature, heat transfer from the warmer surrounding air would occur more quickly. Other examples of thermal insulators in everyday life include vacuum flasks and oven gloves.

Physicist

Product designer

STEM JOBS GLOSSARY

Aerospace engineer

Aerospace engineers design, build and maintain planes, spacecraft and satellites. They have to think carefully about how their designs will impact the environment. Aerospace engineers need to have good mathematical and problem solving skills.

Archaeologist

Archaeologists study human history by examining artefacts and remains from the past such as tools, coins and bones. They discover these objects by carrying out archaeological excavations (digs). Their findings help them to understand more about how people lived in the past.

Architect

Architects design buildings such as homes, schools and hospitals. As well as making buildings look nice, they also need to make sure that they are safe and serve the purpose they were designed for. They work closely with civil engineers to make sure designs are built correctly.

Astronaut

Astronauts go on missions into space, usually working as part of a crew on board a spacecraft. They are likely to need a degree in engineering, science or medicine. Astronaut selection is a tough process that includes physical, mental and academic tests.

Astronomer

Astronomy is the study of the universe beyond the earth, including stars and planets. Astronomers use telescopes and computers to observe distant phenomena, such as black holes or other planets. Their findings can help us to know more about how the universe works and about how it was formed over billions of years.

Biologist

Biologists study living things like animals and plants, which they call organisms. They consider how different organisms have adapted to their environment so that they can survive and successfully reproduce. Biologists specialise in different areas including zoology (the study of animals), botany (the study of plants), human biology and marine biology.

Botanist

Botany is the area of biology that studies plants. As well as identifying plants, botanists also help to conserve and protect them from pests, disease and climate change. Some botanists focus on studying plants that are used for food or medicine.

Chemist

Chemistry is the area of science concerned with how different sorts of atoms join together to form molecules, which are found in living systems (organic chemistry) or non-living systems (inorganic chemistry). Chemists use their knowledge of molecules and the properties of the substances they form to create and improve things like medical treatments and fuels. They often work in laboratories.

Civil engineer

Civil engineers design and oversee the construction of structures such as buildings, roads, railways and bridges. They also help to maintain them and ensure that they are safe to use.

Computer programmer

Computer programmers create instructions for computers to follow. These instructions are called 'code'. They develop, test, maintain and debug (fix) computer programs. Many programmers have a degree in computer science, but it is a skill increasingly learnt by all scientists and engineers.

Cryptographer

Cryptographers analyse and decipher data that has been encrypted (converted into a secret code). They also encrypt data, adding an extra layer of security to make it harder for people who are not meant to have access to it to read it. Cryptographers often work for governments to ensure the safety of their data.

Dendrologist

Dendrology is a branch of science that specialises in the study of woody plants such as trees. Dendrologists know how to identify and categorise different trees. They work to protect woodland environments and spend a lot of time working outdoors.

Doctor

Doctors examine, diagnose and treat disease, illness and injury in human patients. Some doctors work as general practitioners in a local surgery while others work in hospitals, which contain beds and more advanced equipment. Hospital is where people who need longer or more complex care go. Doctors often specialise in a particular area of medicine such as cardiology (the study of the heart) or neurology (the study of the brain and nervous system).

Electrician

Electricians install and maintain electrical systems, including lighting, security and fire safety systems. They work in a variety of buildings, such as homes, schools and factories and on new constructions. A high standard of training is needed to ensure they know how to work safely, as there are a lot of dangers involved with electricity.

Entomologist

Entomologists are biologists who study insects, such as ants, bees, butterflies and beetles. They are interested in their life cycles and behaviour and may observe them in their natural habitats. At other times entomologists collect insects and observe them in laboratories.

Environmental engineer

Environmental engineers design and implement solutions to environmental issues. This includes leading improvements in areas such as recycling, waste disposal, water filtration, air pollution, renewable energy and climate change.

Environmental scientist

Environmental scientists study the impact of human activity on the environment. This includes areas such as air, soil and water pollution. They identify ways to minimise hazards and damage to the environment, such as recycling packaging or using renewable energy.

Forensic scientist

Forensic scientists are responsible for identifying, collecting and analysing physical evidence related to crimes. Their work involves chemistry (e.g. identifying suspected poisons) and biology (e.g. looking for DNA evidence). They often perform this work in laboratories.

Geologist

Geologists study the structure of the earth and its natural resources, and how they have changed over time. This involves analysing rocks, soil, fossils and minerals. They also assess the risk of natural hazards such as volcanoes and earthquakes.

Marine biologist

Marine biologists study life in the oceans. They are also interested in how human activities affect marine life and ways to minimise this impact. Many marine biologists spend a lot of time outdoors, including working on ships or diving underwater to monitor marine life.

Mathematician

Mathematicians either aim to understand the world using logic and abstract concepts (known as 'pure' mathematics) or to solve practical problems by analysing data with statistics and formulas (known as 'applied' mathematics). They often work closely with other experts, such as scientists or engineers, to solve problems.

Mechanical engineer

Mechanical engineers help to research, design, make and maintain a range of machines. These include spacecraft, aircraft, trains and cars. Mechanics is a branch of physics that deals with forces and motion. Mechanical engineers need to have a good understanding of this area to help them do their job.

Meteorologist

Meteorologists study and predict the weather. To do this they collect data about the atmosphere from weather stations and satellites. They use this data to make short-term weather predictions (e.g. it will rain tomorrow), and sometimes long-term climate predictions (e.g. the sea level will rise over the next 50 years).

Naturalist

Naturalists are scientists who study the natural world. In particular they observe how different species of plants and animals interact with each other in their natural habitats.

Physicist

Physicists study the natural universe and use mathematics to explain how the world works. Physicists study different areas including space, atoms, sound and light. They can have wide-ranging careers as they are good at problem solving.

Pilot

Pilots fly planes carrying passengers and cargo on long- and short-haul flights. Larger planes are usually operated by at least two pilots, who take it in turns to fly. Pilots are responsible for the safe operation of the plane and need to be well-prepared and calm in an emergency.

Product designer

Product designers design all sorts of items, from chairs to computers. They have a good eye for detail and use this both to design new products and to improve existing designs. They need to have a good understanding of technology, materials and manufacturing methods, as well as an understanding of style and fashion.

Robotics engineer

Robotics engineers are responsible for designing, building and testing robots. Robots are machines with some degree of artificial intelligence, and can be programmed to perform jobs that are repetitive or too difficult for humans to do. Robots can be found in industries such as manufacturing, retail and agriculture (farming).

Sailor

Sailors work on passenger ships, tankers (which carry liquids and gases in bulk) and freighters (which carry goods). They have various jobs depending on the type of ship, such as safely stowing the ship's cargo, maintaining the ship, helping to navigate and steer the ship and ensuring it arrives safely at the destination.

Seismologist

Seismologists are scientists who study earthquakes and volcanic activity. They use instruments to collect data about seismic waves in the ground or ocean, to better understand the science of earth's shifting tectonic plates. They also monitor this data for unusual patterns. This helps them to give advance warning to people to evacuate from danger areas.

Sound engineer

Sound engineers set up and operate sound equipment. They record and edit sound for a variety of media, including films, video games, music concerts and sporting events. They are often involved in the development and application of new sound technology.

Statistician

Statisticians use numbers to understand problems and identify appropriate solutions. They find clear, visual ways to display information and make it easier to understand, such as using graphs. Sometimes they use statistical models to forecast what might happen in the future (e.g. to the economy or the climate). They need to have good mathematical skills.

Water engineer

Water engineers ensure that humans have a continuous supply of clean water. Their work may involve designing and maintaining water management systems to do jobs such as collecting water in reservoirs and storage tanks, disposing of sewage and preventing floods.

15 FINAL STEM ACTIVITY IDEAS

I hope you've enjoyed the activities in this book and are now bursting with enthusiasm for STEM subjects! Here are 15 more quick and easy ways to nurture your interest in STEM.

1. **Use a magnifying glass to explore.** Search the ground for bugs, take a closer look at the leaves on a tree or hunt for fossils on the beach.

2. **Go stargazing.** Go outside on a clear night and look up at the stars in the sky. Use a night sky app (such as SkyView Lite) to help you identify the different constellations.

3. **Grow your own plants.** Plant seeds such as sunflowers in a pot of soil and leave them in a sunny spot such as a windowsill. You could measure and record their growth each day.

4. **Learn to code.** Websites such as https://scratch.mit.edu/ and https://code.org/ are great places to learn basic coding skills.

5. **Get cooking.** The kitchen is a great place to apply measuring skills. Follow a recipe, measuring out the ingredients accurately.

6. **Take a trip to a local museum or zoo**. This is a great way to not only bring learning to life but also to meet experts in different fields.

7. **Play puzzles and games.** Sudoku and chess are great for developing logical thinking. Construction toys such as wooden or plastic blocks help to develop spatial awareness. Anything involving dice is great for developing mathematical skills.

8. **Create your own board game.** Design a game to share your knowledge about a particular area of STEM. The game could be about space, times tables, the human body … there are so many options!

9. **Go on a number walk.** There are lots of variations of this activity: search for the numbers 1–20, find multiples of a particular times table, hunt for prime numbers …

10. **Build a shelter.** You could create your shelter outside using natural materials like sticks or inside using household items like empty cardboard boxes.

11. **Try origami.** Turning a square of paper into a piece of origami involves a lot of mathematical thinking, including about geometry, fractions and angles.

12. **Take a toy apart to see how it works** (you will need an adult to supervise). Think about how each of the different parts work and then see if you can put the toy back together again.

13. **Transform a box.** From cars to rockets, caves to castles, a box has the potential to be so much more than just a box. Be imaginative and see what you can create.

14. **Read STEM picture books.** There's a whole host of books available that inspire and challenge stereotypes in STEM. See the blogs on my website for ideas: www.howtostem.co.uk.

15. **Download STEM apps.** From coding to virtual reality, there are lots of great STEM apps available, many of which are completely free. Again, there are plenty of ideas blogged on my website: www. howtostem.co.uk.

FURTHER READING FOR ADULTS

Here are some of the books that inspired me to write the 15-Minute STEM series. Although not exclusively about STEM education, they share a focus on developing real-world learning and equipping children with the 'future skills' they will need.

Boaler, Jo (2016). *Mathematical Mindsets: Unleashing Students' Potential through Creative Math, Inspiring Messages and Innovative Teaching* (San Francisco, CA: Jossey-Bass).

Boaler, Jo (2015). *The Elephant in the Classroom: Helping Children Learn and Love Maths* (London: Souvenir Press).

Claxton, Guy (2008). *What's the Point of School? Rediscovering the Heart of Education* (Oxford: Oneworld Publications).

Claxton, Guy and Lucas, Bill (2015). *Educating Ruby: What Our Children Really Need to Learn* (Carmarthen: Crown House Publishing).

Dweck, Carol (2017). *Mindset: Changing the Way You Think to Fulfil Your Potential* (London: Robinson).

Gerver, Richard (2019). *Education: A Manifesto for Change* (London: Bloomsbury).

Gerver, Richard (2014). *Creating Tomorrow's Schools Today*, 2nd edn (London: Bloomsbury).

Illingworth, Martin (2020). *Forget School: Why Young People are Succeeding on their Own Terms and What Schools Can Do to Avoid Being Left Behind* (Carmarthen: Independent Thinking Press).

Lear, Jonathan (2019). *The Monkey-Proof Box: Curriculum Design for Building Knowledge, Developing Creative Thinking and Promoting Independence* (Carmarthen: Independent Thinking Press).

Robinson, Ken and Aronica, Lou (2016). *Creative Schools: The Grassroots Revolution That's Transforming Education* (London: Penguin).

ANSWERS

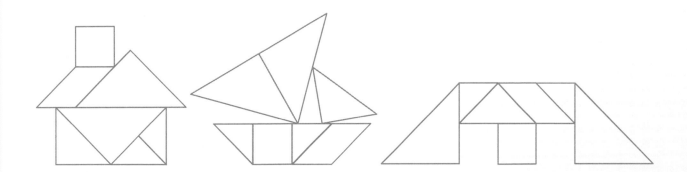

15-MINUTE STEM

Quick, creative Science, Technology, Engineering and Mathematics activities for 5-11-year-olds

Emily Hunt

ISBN: 978-178583335-9

Emily Hunt's *15-Minute STEM: Quick, creative science, technology, engineering and mathematics activities for 5–11-year-olds* offers an exciting collection of 40 tried-and-tested, easy-to-resource STEM activities designed to engage and inspire young learners.

From caring for our environment to the digital revolution, the demand for STEM skills is huge and is only set to grow. STEM is therefore an important priority area in modern education, leaving many teachers and parents asking questions such as 'How do I fit STEM education into my day?' and 'What kind of activities should I be exploring?'

Enter *15-Minute STEM* with the answers …

This innovative resource has been designed to reassure teachers and parents that they don't need to be experts to deliver high-quality STEM education. Each of the 40 activities includes step-by-step instructions, takes just 15 minutes to complete and can be resourced from everyday materials found in the classroom or at home. This means that, with minimal preparation, teachers can slot these cross-curricular activities into an otherwise busy day, broadening their pupils' learning at no cost to their focus on core curriculum areas.

Suitable for both teachers and parents.